Better Homes and Gardens®

CHRISTMAS COOKING
FROM THE HEART™

Spread the Joy

Meredith® Consumer Marketing
Des Moines, Iowa

CHRISTMAS COOKING
FROM THE HEART™

MEREDITH CORPORATION CONSUMER MARKETING
Consumer Marketing Product Director: Heather Sorensen
Consumer Marketing Product Manager: Janece Schwartzkopf
Consumer Marketing Billing/Renewal Manager: Tami Beachem
Business Director: Ron Clingman
Senior Production Manager: Al Rodruck

WATERBURY PUBLICATIONS, INC.
Editorial Director: Lisa Kingsley
Creative Director: Ken Carlson
Associate Editor: Tricia Bergman
Associate Editor/Food Stylist: Annie Peterson
Assistant Food Stylist: Skyler Myers
Associate Design Director: Doug Samuelson
Graphic Designer: Mindy Samuelson
Contributing Copy Editor: Peg Smith
Contributing Proofreader: Terri Fredrickson
Contributing Food Stylist: Jennifer Peterson
Contributing Photographers: Marty Baldwin, Jason Donnelly

***BETTER HOMES AND GARDENS*® MAGAZINE**
Editor in Chief: Stephen Orr
Art Director: Jennifer D. Madara
Senior Deputy Editor: Nancy Wall Hopkins
Editorial Assistant: Renee Irey

MEREDITH NATIONAL MEDIA GROUP
President: Tom Harty

MEREDITH CORPORATION
Chairman and Chief Executive Officer: Stephen M. Lacy

In Memoriam: E.T. Meredith III (1933–2003)

Test Kitchen

Our seal assures you that every recipe in *Christmas Cooking from the Heart*™ has been tested in the *Better Homes and Gardens*® Test Kitchen. This means that each recipe is practical and reliable and it meets our high standards of taste appeal. We guarantee your satisfaction with this book for as long as you own it.

All of us at Meredith® Consumer Marketing are dedicated to providing you with information and ideas to enhance your home. We welcome your comments and suggestions. Write to us at: Meredith Consumer Marketing, 1716 Locust St., Des Moines, IA 50309-3023. *Christmas Cooking from the Heart*™ is available by mail. To order editions from past years, call 800/627-5490.

Cover Photography: Jason Donnelly
Front Cover: Snow Globe Cupcakes (page 78)

UPSIDE-DOWN
GRAPEFRUIT
CAKES, PAGE 144

ROASTED KALE, TOMATO
AND CHICKPEA SALAD WITH
WHEAT BERRIES

Table of Contents

Spread the Joy

Food—central to celebrations—infuses the holidays with the power to make and recall memories—crisp-skinned roasted turkey, savory green bean casserole, warmly spiced gingerbread cookies. These and more special foods draw friends and family together to enjoy one another's company amid familiar dishes and flavors that make the holiday season so special. *Better Homes and Gardens® Christmas Cooking from the Heart™* features recipes tailored to holiday meals—from Thanksgiving through New Year's—and gatherings from formal to super casual. For a big family feast, choose Pineapple-Glazed Pork Roast or Rosemary Olive Roast Beef (page 11). For a celebratory holiday brunch, try Potato-Thyme Frittata (page 44) or Very Cherry Hazelnut Coffee Cake (page 48). For final flourishes, serve decadent desserts—perhaps Snickerdoodle Cheesecake (page 84), Maple Bread Pudding with Pecan Praline (page 85), or Double-Chocolate-Espresso Truffle Pie (page 80).

Happy Cooking—and Happy Holidays!

MEXICAN
CHOCOLATE AND
ESPRESSO CAKE
POPS, PAGE 118

CAULIFLOWER
AU GRATIN, PAGE 18

SPICY GREEN BEAN
CASSEROLE, PAGE 17

Sit-Down Dinner Party

The holiday season is the perfect time to pull out all the culinary stops and create a memory-making meal for family and friends. You'll find all of the elements you need—impressive main dishes, salads, side dishes, and breads—on these pages.

VEGETARIAN SPROUTS
AND MUSHROOM
LASAGNA

VEGETARIAN SPROUTS AND MUSHROOM LASAGNA

PREP 45 minutes
BAKE 55 minutes at 350°F
STAND 40 minutes

- 2 cups raw cashews
- 12 dried lasagna noodles
- 1 15-oz. can pumpkin
- 1 clove garlic
- 1 tsp. salt
- ¼ cup water
- 2 Tbsp. olive oil
- 2 cloves garlic, minced
- 8 oz. cremini mushrooms, sliced
- 8 oz. Brussels sprouts, trimmed and thinly sliced (reserve ½ cup leaves)
- 1 5-oz. bunch kale, stemmed and chopped (5 cups)
- 2 23- to 26-oz. jars marinara sauce (5 cups)
- 8 oz. shredded mozzarella cheese (2 cups)

1. Soak cashews in a bowl of water 30 minutes. Meanwhile, preheat oven to 350°F. Cook noodles according to package directions; drain and rinse with cold water. Drain again and set aside. Drain soaked cashews.

2. In a food processor add pumpkin, cashews, garlic, and salt. Process until nearly smooth. Add the water and process until smooth and spreadable.

3. In a large skillet heat olive oil over medium-high heat. Add garlic; cook 30 seconds or until fragrant. Add mushrooms and Brussels sprouts; cook 5 to 7 minutes or until tender. Add kale, tossing and cooking 2 to 3 minutes or until wilted. Remove from heat.

4. Spread 1 cup of the marinara in a 13×9-inch baking dish. Top with three lasagna noodles, one-third of the pumpkin mixture, one-third of the vegetable mixture, and 1 cup marinara.

Repeat layers twice. Top with remaining lasagna noodles, remaining sauce, and cheese. Cover pan loosely with foil.

5. Bake 45 minutes. Uncover and bake 10 to 15 minutes more or until heated through. Meanwhile, in a medium skillet heat 1 tsp. olive; add reserved Brussels sprout leaves. Cook over medium-high heat 1 minute or until vibrant in color. Sprinkle on baked lasagna; let stand 10 minutes before serving. Makes 12 servings.

PER SERVING *378 cal., 18 g fat (4 g sat. fat), 14 mg chol., 787 mg sodium, 41 g carb., 7 g fiber, 16 g pro.*

ROSEMARY OLIVE ROAST BEEF

PREP 25 minutes
STAND 15 minutes
ROAST 1 hour 30 minutes at 350°F

1	3½- to 4-pound beef sirloin tip roast
2	Tbsp. chopped fresh rosemary
1	Tbsp. kosher salt
2	tsp. freshly ground black pepper
2	Tbsp. olive oil
1	recipe Rosemary Olives Chopped fresh rosemary (optional)

1. Preheat oven to 350°F. Season beef all over with the 2 Tbsp. rosemary, salt, and pepper. In an extra-large skillet heat oil over medium-high heat. Brown roast on all sides. Transfer roast to a rack set in a roasting pan.

2. Roast 1 hour 30 minutes to 1 hour 45 minutes or until a thermometer registers 135°F. Remove from oven. Cover with foil; let stand 15 minutes (temperature of roast will continue to rise). Serve with Rosemary Olives and additional fresh rosemary, if desired. Makes 8 servings.

Rosemary Olives In a large skillet heat 3 Tbsp. oil over medium heat. Add 1½ cups pitted mixed olives; 5 small cloves garlic, peeled and halved lengthwise; 4 small sprigs fresh rosemary; and 4 sprigs fresh thyme. Cook 3 minutes or until herbs begin to sizzle, tossing occasionally to avoid browning the garlic. Season with a pinch of kosher salt, Aleppo or crushed red pepper, and coarse black pepper. Cook 1 minute more. Serve warm spooned over roast beef.

PER SERVING *483 cal., 34 g fat (10 g sat. fat), 146 mg chol., 703 mg sodium, 3 g carb., 1 g fiber, 41 g pro.*

PINEAPPLE-GLAZED PORK ROAST

PREP 25 minutes
CHILL 8 hours
ROAST 15 minutes at 425°F + 40 minutes at 350°F
STAND 10 minutes

8	cups cold water
½	cup kosher salt
¼	cup packed brown sugar
1	3½- to 4-pound natural center cut pork loin roast
4	fresh bay leaves
2	Tbsp. olive oil
1	Tbsp. butter
½	cup whole grain mustard
½	cup packed brown sugar
5	cups chopped fresh pineapple
	Aleppo pepper

1. In a 6- to 8-quart pot stir together the cold water, salt, and brown sugar until dissolved. Add roast and bay leaves. Cover and chill at least 8 hours or up to 48 hours.

2. Preheat oven to 425°F. Remove roast and bay leaves from brine; discard liquid and set bay leaves aside. Pat roast dry with paper towels. In a large skillet heat oil and butter over medium-high heat. Add roast and brown well on all sides. Place in a foil-lined roasting pan. Spread mustard all over roast then pat with brown sugar. Top with pineapple and Aleppo pepper. Roast 15 minutes. Reduce heat to 350°F. Roast 40 to 50 minutes more or until a thermometer registers 145°F, basting once and adding bay leaves after 30 minutes. Cover and let rest 10 minutes. Serve with pan juices and sprinkle with Aleppo pepper. Makes 10 servings.

PER SERVING *379 cal., 17 g fat (6 g sat. fat), 112 mg chol., 517 mg sodium, 21 g carb., 1 g fiber, 33 g pro.*

PINEAPPLE-GLAZED PORK ROAST

PEACH-GLAZED ROAST TURKEY

PREP 20 minutes
ROAST 3 hours at 325°F
COOK 40 minutes
STAND 15 minutes

1   14- to 18-pound turkey
     Salt and black pepper
1   peach, peeled, seeded, and
     quartered, or 1 cup frozen peach
     slices, thawed
1   lemon, quartered
5   fresh thyme sprigs
5   fresh rosemary sprigs
4   Tbsp. butter
1   cup finely chopped yellow onion
1   cup peach preserves
1   cup orange juice
½   cup cider vinegar
2   tsp. dry mustard
1   tsp. salt

1. For the turkey, preheat oven to 325°F. Remove neck and giblets; reserve for another use or discard. Rinse body cavity; pat dry with paper towels. Place turkey on a rack in a roasting pan. Generously season cavity with salt and pepper. Stuff with peach, lemon quarters, thyme, and rosemary. Tie drumsticks together with 100%-cotton kitchen string. Twist wing tips under back. Melt 2 Tbsp. of the butter. Brush turkey with melted butter then generously season with salt and pepper. Roast 2½ hours.
2. Meanwhile, for peach glaze, melt remaining 2 Tbsp. butter in a small saucepan over medium heat. Add onion and cook 4 minutes or until tender. Add preserves, orange juice, vinegar, mustard, and 1 tsp. salt. Bring to boiling; reduce heat and boil gently, uncovered, 35 minutes or until thickened, stirring occasionally.
3. Cut string on drumsticks. Roast 1¼ hours to 1¾ hours or until a thermometer registers 175°F when inserted deep into a thigh (away from bone), brushing with ½ cup of the peach glaze the last 20 minutes of roasting. Cover turkey loosely with foil during roasting, if necessary, to prevent overbrowning. Remove turkey, cover with foil, and let rest 15 minutes before carving. Serve with remaining peach glaze. Makes 10 servings.
PER SERVING *559 cal., 21 g fat (6 g sat. fat), 239 mg chol., 803 mg sodium, 19 g carb., 1 g fiber, 70 g pro.*

CREAMY GRAVY

PREP 10 minutes

3   Tbsp. turkey drippings, butter, or
     bacon drippings
1¾   cups milk
3   Tbsp. all-purpose flour
¼   tsp. salt
⅛   tsp. black pepper

1. Heat drippings in large skillet over medium heat. In a screw-top jar combine ¾ cup of the milk, the flour, salt, and pepper; cover and shake until well combined. Add milk mixture to skillet. Whisk in remaining 1 cup milk. Cook, stirring constantly, until thickened and bubbly. Cook and stir 1 minute more. Reduce heat if gravy bubbles vigorously. If desired, thin with additional milk. Makes 2 cups or 8 servings.
PER SERVING *108 cal., 8 g fat (3 g sat. fat), 12 mg chol., 140 mg sodium, 6 g carb., 0 g fiber, 3 g pro.*

PEAR-CRANBERRY CHUTNEY

START TO FINISH 25 minutes

1   12-oz. bag fresh cranberries
1   small onion, chopped
1   cup packed brown sugar
½   cup water
3   Tbsp. lemon juice
1   inch piece fresh ginger, grated
¼   tsp. ground cinnamon
⅛   tsp. ground cloves
     Dash cayenne pepper
3   Bosc pears, cored and chopped
     Chopped walnuts (optional)

1. In a medium saucepan combine all ingredients except pears and walnuts. Bring to boiling; reduce heat. Simmer, uncovered, 10 minutes or until cranberries soften. Add pears and cook 5 to 10 minutes longer or until pears are soft yet keep their texture. Serve chilled or at room temperature. Top with chopped walnuts, if desired. Makes 16 servings.
PER SERVING *83 cal., 0 g fat, 0 mg chol., 5 mg sodium, 22 g carb., 2 g fiber, 0 g pro.*

WHIPPED FRESH HERB BUTTER

PREP 15 minutes

1   cup heavy cream
2   Tbsp. assorted fresh herbs (such as
     rosemary, oregano, basil, chives,
     parsley, and/or thyme)
¼   tsp. sea salt

1. In a large bowl beat cream with a mixer on low 2 minutes or until cream starts to thicken. Increase to medium and beat 6 to 8 minutes. Cream will first beat to stiff peaks, then butter clumps will form and a milky liquid will appear in bowl. Scrape sides as needed.
2. When clumps form and no more liquid is released, transfer mixture to a fine-mesh sieve set over a bowl. Using the back of a spoon, gently press out excess liquid. Discard liquid.
3. Transfer to a small bowl. Stir in herbs and salt. Store, covered, in the refrigerator up to 5 days. Makes 8 servings.
PER SERVING *108 cal., 8 g fat (3 g sat. fat), 12 mg chol., 140 mg sodium, 6 g carb., 0 g fiber, 3 g pro.*

PEAR-CRANBERRY CHUTNEY

MASHED SWEET POTATOES
WITH MUSHROOMS AND BACON

CREAMY HORSERADISH MASHED POTATOES

PREP 30 minutes
COOK 20 minutes

- 3 lbs. russet, Yukon gold, or red potatoes, peeled if desired and cut into 2-inch pieces
- ¼ cup butter
- ¼ to ⅓ cup milk, heavy cream, half-and-half, or light cream
- ¼ cup sour cream
- 1 to 2 Tbsp. prepared horseradish
- 1 tsp. lemon juice
- 1 tsp. salt
- ½ tsp. freshly cracked black pepper
  Melted butter (optional)

1. In a 4- to 5-quart Dutch oven cook potatoes, covered, in enough lightly salted boiling water to cover 20 to 25 minutes or until tender; drain. Return potatoes to Dutch oven. Add the ¼ cup butter. Let stand, uncovered, 2 to 3 minutes. Meanwhile, in a small saucepan warm the milk over low heat until hot but not boiling.
2. Mash potatoes with a potato masher or beat with mixer on low just until light and fluffy. Stir in warm milk, sour cream, horseradish, lemon juice, salt, and pepper. Gradually stir in additional milk to reach desired consistency. Sprinkle with cracked black pepper and, if desired, top with melted butter. Makes 10 servings.

PER SERVING 118 cal., 5 g fat (3 g sat. fat), 13 mg chol., 296 mg sodium, 17 g carb., 2 g fiber, 2 g pro.

MASHED SWEET POTATOES WITH MUSHROOMS AND BACON

START TO FINISH 30 minutes

- 3 lb. orange-flesh sweet potatoes, peeled and cut up
- ½ cup milk
- 2 Tbsp. butter
- 1 tsp. kosher salt
- 6 slices bacon
- 8 oz. cremini mushrooms, halved (quarter large mushrooms)
- 1 large onion, cut in thin wedges
- 2 Tbsp. lemon juice
- ⅓ cup golden raisins

1. In a 4- to 5-quart Dutch oven cook potatoes in lightly salted boiling water, covered, 20 to 25 minutes or until tender. Drain; return to pan. Using a potato masher, mash potatoes. Stir in milk, butter, and salt until butter is melted. Cover and keep warm.
2. Meanwhile, in a large skillet cook bacon over medium heat 8 to 10 minutes until crisp. Transfer to paper towels, reserving 3 Tbsp. drippings in skillet. Add mushrooms and onion to skillet. Cook and stir over medium heat 8 minutes or until

mushrooms are tender and browned. Drizzle with lemon juice. Crumble bacon and stir into mushrooms along with raisins. Top mashed potatoes with warm mushroom mixture. Makes 10 servings.
PER SERVING 196 cal., 8 g fat (4 g sat. fat), 15 mg chol., 364 mg sodium, 27 g carb., 4 g fiber, 5 g pro.

ALMOND-SAUSAGE STUFFING

PREP 30 minutes
SLOW COOK 3 hours 30 minutes (low)

- ¼ cup butter, melted
- 3 cups desired combination of onion, mushrooms, and celery
- ¼ cup snipped fresh sage or 2 tsp. dried sage, crushed
- ¼ tsp. black pepper
- 12 cups dry corn bread cubes*
- 1 cup cooked bulk pork sausage (optional)
- 1 14.5-oz. can reduced-sodium chicken broth
- 1 cup chopped roasted almonds (optional)
  Reduced-sodium chicken broth (optional)

1. In a large skillet cook onion, mushrooms, and celery in melted butter over medium heat 5 minutes or until tender, stirring occasionally. Remove from heat. Stir in sage and pepper.
2. Line a 6-quart slow cooker with a disposable slow cooker liner. Place bread cubes and, if desired, sausage in cooker. Add cooked vegetables. Drizzle with enough broth to moisten; lightly toss.
3. Cook, covered, on low 3½ to 4 hours. If desired, gently stir in almonds. If needed, stir in enough additional warmed broth to reach desired consistency. Makes 10 servings.
*Cut fresh corn bread into 1-inch cubes. Preheat oven to 300°F. Spread cubes in two 15×10-inch baking pans. Bake 10 to 15 minutes or until dry, stirring twice; cool. (Cubes continue to dry and crisp as they cool.) Or let bread cubes stand, loosely covered, at room temperature 8 to 12 hours.
PER SERVING 411 cal., 15 g fat (7 g sat. fat), 74 mg chol., 810 mg sodium, 61 g carb., 3 g fiber, 8 g pro.

SPICY GREEN
BEAN
CASSEROLE

SPICY GREEN BEAN CASSEROLE

PREP 45 minutes
BAKE 12 minutes at 475°F

5   Tbsp. unsalted butter
1   Tbsp. vegetable oil
1   cup panko bread crumbs
2   Tbsp. slivered almonds
12   oz. cremini and/or shiitake mushrooms, sliced
½   cup thinly sliced onion
1   tsp. minced fresh serrano or jalapeño peppers (tip, page 29)
4   cloves garlic, minced
1   tsp. plus 1 Tbsp. kosher salt
2   Tbsp. all-purpose flour
1   tsp. ground chipotle chile pepper
½   tsp. ground white pepper
¼   tsp. ground nutmeg
1   bay leaf
1   cup chicken stock or broth
1   cup half-and-half or light cream
1   lb. fresh haricot verts (French string beans), rinsed, trimmed, and halved

1. For crumb topping, in a small saucepan melt 2 Tbsp. of the butter and the oil together; stir in panko and almonds. Cook and stir over medium-low heat 4 to 6 minutes until golden brown. Place on a paper towel-lined tray.
2. In a medium heavy skillet melt the remaining 3 Tbsp. butter over medium heat. Add mushrooms, onion, serrano, garlic, and 1 tsp. of the salt. Cook 3 to 6 minutes or until mushrooms release moisture and onions are tender, stirring occasionally. Add flour, chipotle, white pepper, nutmeg, and bay leaf; cook and stir 2 minutes more. Add stock and half-and-half; bring to a simmer. Simmer, uncovered, 7 to 10 minutes or until thickened, stirring occasionally. Remove and discard bay leaf. Remove from heat.
3. Preheat oven to 475°F. In a large pot bring water to boiling with 1 Tbsp. salt. Add beans; cook 4 to 6 minutes. Drain then submerge in a large bowl of ice water. Drain again. Add beans to cream mixture then place in a 2-quart baking dish.
4. Bake, uncovered, 12 to 15 minutes or until bubbly. Remove from oven. Sprinkle with crumb topping. Makes 10 servings.
PER SERVING 157 cal., 11 g fat (6 g sat. fat), 24 mg chol., 344 mg sodium, 12 g carb., 2 g fiber, 4 g pro.

SWEET CORN RISOTTO WITH BASIL AND BACON

PREP 20 minutes
SLOW COOK 1 hour (high)

6   slices bacon (not maple-flavor)
4½   cups reduced-sodium chicken broth
½   cup finely chopped Vidalia or other sweet onion
½   cup dry white wine or reduced-sodium chicken broth
2   cups arborio rice
2   cups fresh or frozen sweet corn kernels
½   tsp. salt
2   Tbsp. butter, softened
½   cup packed fresh basil leaves cut into narrow strips

1. In a large skillet cook bacon until crisp; drain on paper towels, reserving 2 Tbsp. drippings in skillet. Crumble bacon. Set aside.
2. Meanwhile, in a medium saucepan bring broth to boiling; reduce heat to simmer.
3. Add onion to reserved drippings in skillet; cook and stir over medium heat 4 minutes or until tender. Add wine; bring to boiling. Reduce heat; simmer, uncovered, 2 minutes, stirring to scrape up any browned bits from bottom of skillet. Stir in rice. Transfer to a 4- to 5-quart slow cooker. Stir in warm broth, corn, and salt.
4. Cover and cook on high 1 to 1¼ hours or until rice is tender and liquid is absorbed, stirring once. Stir in butter. Top with crumbled bacon and basil. Makes 6 servings.
PER SERVING 395 cal., 12 g fat (5 g sat. fat), 23 mg chol., 797 mg sodium, 59 g carb., 2 g fiber, 11 g pro.

SWEET CORN
RISOTTO WITH
BASIL AND BACON

SOUTHWEST CORN PUDDING

PREP 25 minutes
BAKE 30 minutes at 350°F

1 Tbsp. olive oil
1 Tbsp. butter
1 medium onion, halved and thinly sliced
1½ cups frozen whole kernel corn, thawed
½ cup chopped red sweet pepper
½ tsp. ground cumin
¼ cup cornmeal
2 Tbsp. all-purpose flour
½ tsp. salt
1 14.5-oz. can cream-style corn
4 eggs, lightly beaten
1 4-oz. can diced green chiles, undrained
1 cup shredded sharp cheddar cheese (4 oz.)
1 Tbsp. butter

1. Preheat oven to 350°F. In a large cast-iron or other heavy oven-going skillet heat oil and 1 Tbsp. butter over medium-high heat until butter begins to bubble. Add onion; cook 5 minutes or until onion is soft and begins to brown, stirring occasionally. Add corn kernels, sweet pepper, and cumin. Cook and stir 3 minutes. Remove skillet from heat.

2. Meanwhile, in a medium bowl combine cornmeal, flour, and salt. Add cream-style corn, eggs, undrained chiles, and cheese; stir just until combined.

3. Fold onion mixture into cornmeal mixture. Return skillet to medium heat and melt 1 Tbsp. butter, tilting skillet to coat bottom. Pour batter into skillet.

4. Transfer skillet to oven. Bake 30 to 35 minutes or until a knife inserted near center comes out clean. Serve warm. Makes 10 servings.

PER SERVING *183 cal., 10 g fat (5 g sat. fat), 92 mg chol., 389 mg sodium, 18 g carb., 1 g fiber, 8 g pro.*

CAULIFLOWER AU GRATIN

PREP 25 minutes
BAKE 15 minutes at 425°F

1 cup panko bread crumbs
¾ cup finely shredded white cheddar cheese
2 Tbsp. snipped fresh Italian parsley
2 tsp. snipped fresh thyme
1½ tsp. orange zest
1 large head cauliflower, cut into small florets (about 6 cups)
2 Tbsp. olive oil
2 Tbsp. Dijon mustard
¼ to ½ tsp. salt
2 Tbsp. butter, melted
¼ cup chopped, roasted almonds

1. Preheat oven to 425°F. In a bowl combine panko, cheese, parsley, thyme, and orange zest; set aside.

2. In a 4-quart pot bring lightly salted water to boil over high heat. Add cauliflower; reduce heat to medium. Cook 4 minutes or until tender yet firm. Drain well. In a large bowl combine olive oil, mustard, and salt. Add cauliflower and stir gently to coat*.

3. Transfer cauliflower to a 1½- to 2-quart gratin or rectangular baking dish. Sprinkle with panko mixture. Drizzle with melted butter.

4. Bake 15 minutes or until heated through and lightly browned. Top with almonds. Makes 6 servings.

* At this point, separate cauliflower and panko mixtures can be covered and chilled up to 1 day. Remove from refrigerator 45 minutes before baking; continue with Step 3.

PER SERVING *326 cal., 16 g fat (6 g sat. fat), 25 mg chol., 370 mg sodium, 40 g carb., 3 g fiber, 7 g pro.*

BACON-ROASTED BRUSSELS SPROUTS

PREP 15 minutes
ROAST 20 minutes at 400°F

2 slices bacon, chopped
⅛ tsp. crushed red pepper
2 lb. Brussels sprouts, trimmed
½ cup thin wedges red onion
2 tsp. fresh thyme leaves
¼ tsp. salt

1. Preheat oven to 400°F. In an extra-large cast-iron or other heavy oven-going skillet cook and stir bacon over medium heat until bacon is browned and crisp. Place bacon on paper towels to drain. Add crushed red pepper to drippings; cook and stir 1 minute or until fragrant.

2. If Brussels sprouts are large, halve lengthwise. Add sprouts, onion, thyme, and salt to skillet. Stir to coat with drippings. Transfer skillet to oven and roast, uncovered, 20 to 25 minutes or just until tender and browned, stirring once.

3. Transfer sprouts and onion to a serving dish and sprinkle with reserved bacon. Makes 8 servings.

PER SERVING *93 cal., 4 g fat (1 g sat. fat), 6 mg chol., 164 mg sodium, 11 g carb., 5 g fiber, 5 g pro.*

CAULIFLOWER AU GRATIN

BACON-ROASTED
BRUSSELS SPROUTS

WILD RICE WITH PECANS AND CHERRIES

WILD RICE WITH PECANS AND CHERRIES

PREP 20 minutes
SLOW COOK 5 hours (low)
STAND 10 minutes

3   14.5-oz. cans reduced-sodium chicken broth
2½ cups uncooked wild rice, rinsed and drained
1   cup coarsely shredded carrot
1   4-oz. can (drained weight) sliced mushrooms, drained
1   Tbsp. butter
2   tsp. dried marjoram, crushed
¼   tsp. black pepper
⅔   cup chopped green onions
½   cup dried tart cherries
½   cup coarsely chopped pecans, toasted*

1. In a 3½- or 4-quart slow cooker combine first seven ingredients (through pepper). Cover and cook on low 5 to 6 hours.
2. Turn off cooker. Stir in ⅔ cup green onions, dried cherries, and pecans. Cover and let stand 10 minutes. If desired, top servings with additional chopped green onions. Makes 15 servings.
*Tip To toast whole nuts, large pieces of nuts, or coconut, spread them in a shallow pan. Bake at 350°F for 5 to 10 minutes or until toasted or golden, stirring once or twice and watching closely to prevent burning. Toast seeds, finely chopped or ground nuts, or coconut, in a dry skillet over medium heat until lightly toasted or golden brown.
PER SERVING 157 cal., 4 g fat (1 g sat. fat), 2 mg chol., 235 mg sodium, 27 g carb., 3 g fiber, 6 g pro.

KALE SALAD WITH DATES

START TO FINISH 35 minutes

1½ lb. kale, stemmed and chopped (about 15 cups)
5   Tbsp. lemon juice
1¼ tsp. kosher salt
¼   cup extra-virgin olive oil
1   shallot, minced
2   Tbsp. honey
½   tsp. crushed red pepper
1   cup pecan halves, toasted and chopped (tip, above)
1   large Honeycrisp apple, quartered, cored, and sliced
3   oz. Pecorino Romano cheese, shaved
½   cup pitted dates, chopped

1. Rinse and dry kale; place in a large salad bowl. Pour 3 Tbsp. lemon juice and ¼ tsp. of the salt over kale and massage leaves gently for 4 to 5 minutes to tenderize them.
2. Combine olive oil, shallot, honey, 2 Tbsp. lemon juice, remaining salt, and crushed red pepper in a screw-top jar. Shake well.
3. Toss kale with pecans, apple, cheese, and dates. Add dressing and toss to coat. Makes 24 servings.
PER SERVING 105 cal., 7 g fat (1 g sat. fat), 4 mg chol., 125 mg sodium, 10 g carb., 2 g fiber, 3 g pro.

SPICED PECAN APPLE SALAD

PREP 15 minutes
BAKE 10 minutes at 350°F

1⅔ cups pecan pieces
3   Tbsp. butter
1   tsp. ground cinnamon
½   tsp. salt
¼   tsp. cayenne pepper
½   cup extra-virgin olive oil
2   Tbsp. sherry wine vinegar
1   Tbsp. Dijon mustard
1   large red apple, cored and chopped
2   tsp. lemon juice
1   head red leaf lettuce, torn into bite-size pieces
1   cup crumbled feta cheese (8 oz.) Bibb or Boston lettuce leaves Cracked black pepper (optional)

1. For pecans, preheat oven to 350°F. Line a 15×10×1-inch baking pan with foil. Spread pecans in a single layer. In a small saucepan heat butter, cinnamon, salt, and cayenne pepper over low heat until melted, stirring occasionally. Drizzle butter mixture over pecans; stir to coat. Bake 10 to 15 minutes or until pecans are golden brown. Cool in pan on wire rack.
2. For vinaigrette, in a screw-top jar combine oil, vinegar, and mustard. Cover and shake well; set aside.
3. Place chopped apple in a large bowl. Sprinkle with lemon juice; stir gently to coat. Add leaf lettuce and feta cheese; toss to combine. Shake vinaigrette; drizzle over salad and toss to coat. Line salad plates with Bibb lettuce leaves. Top with salad, sprinkle with spiced pecans, and, if desired, season with cracked black pepper. Makes 8 servings.
PER SERVING 385 cal., 38 g fat (9 g sat. fat), 28 mg chol., 442 mg sodium, 8 g carb., 3 g fiber, 6 g pro.

SPICED PECAN
APPLE SALAD

CRIMSON SLAW

WHOLE-LEAF
SALAD

CRIMSON SLAW

PREP 25 minutes
CHILL 2 hours

⅓   cup olive oil
2   Tbsp. sugar
2   Tbsp. red wine vinegar
2   Tbsp. dry red wine
1   tsp. salt
½   tsp. ground black pepper
¼   tsp. dry mustard
4   cups shredded red cabbage
     (½ medium head)
1   6-oz. pkg. dried cranberries
¼   medium red onion, thinly sliced

1. For vinaigrette, in a screw-top jar combine first seven ingredients (through mustard). Cover and shake well.
2. In a large bowl toss together cabbage, cranberries, and onion. Pour vinaigrette over slaw; toss gently to coat. Cover and chill 2 to 24 hours. Makes 6 servings.
PER SERVING *227 cal., 12 g fat (2 g sat. fat), 0 mg chol., 402 mg sodium, 32 g carb., 3 g fiber, 1 g pro.*

WHOLE-LEAF SALAD

START TO FINISH 30 minutes

2   cloves garlic, halved, green
     sprouts removed
1   tsp. kosher salt
¼   cup red wine vinegar
1   tsp. honey
1   tsp. Dijon mustard
¼   tsp. freshly ground black pepper
¾   cup extra-virgin olive oil
¼   cup chopped curly parsley
1   head radicchio, separated into
     leaves (5 cups)
1   head Bibb lettuce, firm inner leaves
     only (5 cups)
1   to 2 heads Belgian endive,
     separated into leaves (2½ cups)
1   bunch arugula (2 cups)
1   bunch curly parsley, leaves and
     tender parts only (2 cups)

1. Chop garlic with salt and rub to a paste with the side of a chef's knife. Transfer to a small bowl and whisk together with vinegar. Let stand 15 minutes. Whisk in honey, mustard, and pepper. Gradually whisk in oil to incorporate. Stir in chopped parsley.
2. Arrange radicchio, Bibb lettuce, Belgian endive, arugula, and parsley sprigs in a serving bowl. Drizzle with dressing. Makes 8 servings.
PER SERVING *205 cal., 21 g fat (3 g sat. fat), 0 mg chol., 177 mg sodium, 5 g carb., 2 g fiber, 2 g pro.*

3 Tbsp. butter or vegetable oil
3 Tbsp. Dijon mustard
1 tsp. salt
1 cup shredded sharp cheddar
   cheese (4 oz.)
2 eggs
   Honey (optional)

1. In a large bowl combine 1½ cups of the flour, the cornmeal, and yeast; set aside. In a small saucepan combine buttermilk, sugar, butter, mustard, and salt. Heat and stir just until warm (120°F to 130°F). Add buttermilk mixture, cheese, and eggs to flour mixture.
2. Beat with a mixer on low to medium 30 seconds, scraping sides of bowl constantly. Beat on high 3 minutes. Stir in as much remaining flour as you can.
3. Turn dough out onto a lightly floured surface. Knead in enough remaining flour to make a moderately stiff dough that is smooth and elastic (6 to 8 minutes total). Shape into a ball. Place dough in a large lightly greased bowl, turning once to grease surface. Cover; let rise in a warm place until double in size (about 1½ hours).
4. Punch dough down. Turn dough out onto a lightly floured surface. Divide dough in half. Cover; let rest 10 minutes. Meanwhile, lightly grease twenty-four 2½-inch muffin cups.
5. Divide each dough half into 36 portions. Shape each portion into a ball, pulling edges under to make a smooth top. Place three balls, smooth sides up, in each prepared muffin cup. Cover muffin pans. (To serve today, let rise in a warm place until nearly double in size [about 45 minutes]. Omit Step 6 and continue as directed in Step 7.)
6. Chill at least 4 hours or up to 24 hours. Uncover; let stand at room temperature 30 minutes before baking.
7. Preheat oven to 375°F. Bake 15 minutes or until rolls sound hollow when lightly tapped. Immediately remove from muffin cups; cool slightly on wire racks. Serve warm with honey, if desired. Makes 24 servings.
*Tip For 1¼ cups sour milk, place 4 tsp. lemon juice or vinegar in a glass measuring cup. Add enough milk to equal 1¼ cups; stir. Let stand 5 minutes before using.
PER SERVING *149 cal., 4 g fat (2 g sat. fat), 27 mg chol., 199 mg sodium, 22 g carb., 1 g fiber, 5 g pro.*

ROASTED GRAPE AND ROSEMARY SCONES

PREP 15 minutes
BAKE 33 minutes at 400°F

1½ cups seedless green grapes
2½ cups all-purpose flour
2   Tbsp. sugar
1   Tbsp. baking powder
¼   tsp. salt
6   Tbsp. butter
1   egg, lightly beaten
1   8-oz. carton crème fraîche
¼   cup heavy cream
1   Tbsp. coarsely chopped fresh
    rosemary

1. Preheat oven to 400°F. Place grapes in a shallow ungreased baking pan. Roast, uncovered, 20 to 25 minutes or until browned and starting to burst; set aside.
2. In a large bowl combine flour, sugar, baking powder, and salt. Using a pastry blender, cut in butter until mixture resembles coarse crumbs. Make a well in center of flour mixture; set aside.
3. In a medium bowl combine egg, crème fraîche, and cream. Add egg mixture all at once to flour mixture. Add roasted grapes and rosemary. Using a fork, stir just until moistened.
4. Turn dough out onto a lightly floured surface. Knead dough by folding and gently pressing 10 to 12 strokes or until dough is nearly smooth. Pat dough into a 10×4-inch rectangle. Cut in half lengthwise and in sixths crosswise to make 12 rectangles.
5. Place rectangles 2 inches apart on ungreased baking sheet. Brush with additional cream. Bake 13 to 15 minutes or until golden brown. Remove scones from baking sheet. Serve warm. Makes 12 servings.
PER SERVING *267 cal., 17 g fat (10 g sat. fat), 68 mg chol., 232 mg sodium, 26 g carb., 1 g fiber, 4 g pro.*

CHEDDAR-CORNMEAL ROLLS

PREP 45 minutes
RISE 1 hour 30 minutes
REST 10 minutes
CHILL 4 hours
STAND 30 minutes
BAKE 15 minutes at 375°F

4   to 4½ cups all-purpose flour
¾   cup cornmeal
2   pkg. active dry yeast
1¼ cups buttermilk or sour milk*
¼   cup sugar

ROASTED GRAPE AND ROSEMARY SCONES

CHEDDAR-CORNMEAL
ROLLS

Holiday Soirée

There is something for everyone in a buffet of party-perfect finger foods. A spread of sweet and spicy wings, meatballs, crostini, and savory tarts (Maple-Bacon Cheesecake Bites) allows guests to nibble and nosh while they circulate and socialize.

FETA CROSTINI WITH TOMATO, BACON, AND APPLE JAM, PAGE 35

FIG AND GORGONZOLA
STUFFED PORK TENDERLOIN

FIG AND GORGONZOLA STUFFED PORK TENDERLOIN

PREP 30 minutes
ROAST 30 minutes at 425°F
STAND 10 minutes

- 2   14- to 18-oz. pork tenderloins
- 1¼   cups crumbled Gorgonzola cheese (5 oz.)
- ¾   cup dried figs, snipped
- ½   cup walnuts, toasted and coarsely chopped
- 1   tsp. salt
- 1   tsp. black pepper
- 2   Tbsp. apple jelly

1. Preheat oven to 425°F. Line a 15×10×1-inch baking pan with foil. Place a rack in the foil-lined pan. Trim fat from meat. Make a lengthwise cut along center of each tenderloin, cutting almost to, but not through, opposite side. Spread open. Using a meat mallet, flatten each tenderloin between two pieces of plastic wrap to about ½-inch thickness.
2. Top each tenderloin with cheese, figs, and walnuts to within ½ inch of edges. From a long side, roll up each tenderloin into a spiral. Tie at 2-inch intervals with 100%-cotton kitchen string. Sprinkle rolls with salt and pepper. Place on rack in prepared baking pan.
3. Roast, uncovered, 20 minutes. Meanwhile, in a small saucepan stir jelly over low heat just until melted. Brush melted jelly over meat rolls. Roast, uncovered, 10 minutes or until meat temperature reaches 145°F. Remove from oven. Cover meat loosely with foil; let stand 10 minutes before slicing. (Temperature of meat will rise 5°F during stand time.) Remove string. Cut each roll into 10 to 12 slices. Serve warm. Makes 20 servings.
PER SERVING *112 cal., 5 g fat (2 g sat. fat), 32 mg chol., 254 mg sodium, 6 g carb., 1 g fiber, 11 g pro.*

SWEET AND SPICY PARTY WINGS

PREP 35 minutes
BAKE 30 minutes at 450°F

- 6   lb. chicken wings tips, discarded, and wings split (about 24)
- 4   cloves garlic, thinly sliced

SWEET AND SPICY PARTY WINGS

- ½   cup unsalted butter, melted
- ½   cup honey
- ¼   cup bottled green hot pepper sauce
- 3   Tbsp. grated fresh ginger
- 1   tsp. kosher salt
- 4   jalapeño peppers,* seeded and chopped

1. Preheat oven to 450°F. Line two 15×10×1-inch baking pans with nonstick foil; set aside. Cut off and discard tips of chicken wings. Cut wings at joints to form about 48 pieces.
2. Bring a large pot of heavily salted water to boiling. Add chicken pieces and garlic. Simmer, uncovered, 8 minutes; drain. Pat chicken wing pieces dry with paper towels then place on prepared baking pans. Bake on separate oven racks 30 minutes or until done (170°F), rotating pans halfway through baking.
3. Meanwhile for sauce, in a small saucepan stir together butter, honey, hot pepper sauce, ginger, and kosher salt. Bring to boiling. Reduce heat and simmer, uncovered, 4 minutes or until sauce is slightly thickened, stirring occasionally.
4. Place wings in a large serving bowl. Add honey sauce; toss to coat. Sprinkle jalapeños over wings. Makes 10 servings.
Tip Chile peppers contain oils that can irritate skin and eyes. Wear plastic or rubber gloves when working with them.
PER SERVING *375 cal., 24 g fat (11 g sat. fat), 164 mg chol., 380 mg sodium, 15 g carb., 0 g fiber, 22 g pro.*

SAUSAGES IN BOURBON-HONEY BARBECUE SAUCE

PREP 25 minutes

1 18-oz. bottle barbecue sauce (1⅔ cups)
¼ cup bourbon
2 Tbsp. Dijon mustard
2 14-oz. links smoked sausage, sliced ½-inch thick
   Bite-size sweet pepper, fresh pineapple, and/or dill pickle chips

1. In a large skillet combine barbecue sauce, bourbon, and mustard. Cook and stir over medium heat until bubbly. Stir in smoked sausage slices. Cook, covered, over medium-low heat 15 minutes or until heated through, stirring occasionally.
2. Serve sausages with sweet pepper, pineapple, and/or pickles. Makes 16 servings.
PER SERVING *223 cal., 14 g fat (5 g sat. fat), 30 mg chol., 820 mg sodium, 15 g carb., 1 g fiber, 6 g pro.*

SRIRACHA PORK MEATBALLS

START TO FINISH 35 minutes

1 egg, lightly beaten
¼ cup fine dry bread crumbs
¼ cup sliced green onions
1 clove garlic, minced
1 tsp. grated fresh ginger
3 Tbsp. reduced-sodium soy sauce
2 Tbsp. sriracha sauce
1 lb. ground pork
1 Tbsp. vegetable oil
¾ cup ketchup
¼ cup packed brown sugar
1 Tbsp. toasted sesame oil
1 Tbsp. rice vinegar
2 Tbsp. chopped fresh cilantro
2 tsp. sesame seeds, toasted (tip, page 20)

1. In a bowl combine egg, bread crumbs, green onions, garlic, ginger, and 1 Tbsp. soy sauce and 1 Tbsp. sriracha. Add ground pork; mix well. Shape into 18 meatballs. In a large skillet cook meatballs, half at a time, in hot vegetable oil over medium heat 5 minutes, turning occasionally. Remove meatballs from skillet; drain off fat.
2. Meanwhile, for sauce, in a bowl stir together ketchup, brown sugar, remaining 2 Tbsp. soy sauce, remaining 1 Tbsp. sriracha, sesame oil, and rice vinegar. Add to skillet and stir over medium heat until bubbly, scraping up any browned bits. Return meatballs to skillet. Reduce heat; cover and cook 5 minutes. Uncover; cook 5 minutes more or until meatballs are done (160°F), turning occasionally. Sprinkle with cilantro and sesame seeds. Makes 18 servings.
PER SERVING *107 cal., 6 g fat (2 g sat. fat), 27 mg chol., 237 mg sodium, 8 g carb., 5 g pro.*

SRIRACHA PORK MEATBALLS

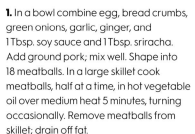

CHILLED WHITE WINE, GINGER, AND SERRANO SCALLOPS WITH VEGETABLES

PREP 30 minutes
CHILL 2 hours

- 1 lime
- 1 cup water
- ½ cup dry white wine
- ⅓ cup finely chopped red onion
- 1 serrano pepper, seeded and finely chopped (tip, page 29)
- 1½ lb. bay scallops
- ½ cup finely chopped red sweet pepper
- ½ cup chopped seedless cucumber
- ½ cup chopped seeded tomato
- 6 radishes, halved and thinly sliced
- ¼ cup dry white wine
- 3 Tbsp. olive oil
- 1 tsp. grated fresh ginger
- ½ tsp. kosher salt
- ¼ tsp. black pepper
- ⅓ cup coarsely chopped cilantro

1. Using a vegetable peeler, remove two strips of lime zest (about 1×3 inches each) and 2 Tbsp. juice from lime. Set juice aside. In a medium saucepan combine zest strips, the water, wine, onion, and the serrano pepper. Heat over medium-high heat until mixture just comes to a boil. Add scallops; gently stir. Remove from heat. Cover and let stand 2 minutes. Drain scallops, discarding liquid. Transfer to a bowl and drizzle with lime juice. Cover and refrigerate 2 hours or until chilled.
2. In a bowl stir together red pepper, cucumber, tomato, radishes, white wine, olive oil, ginger, salt, and pepper. Cover and chill until ready to serve or up to 8 hours. Stir scallops into vegetables and sprinkle with cilantro. Makes 32 servings.
PER SERVING *31 cal., 1 g fat (0 g sat. fat), 5 mg chol., 103 mg sodium, 2 g carb., 0 g fiber, 3 g pro.*

CHILLED WHITE WINE, GINGER, AND SERRANO SCALLOPS WITH VEGETABLES

MAPLE BACON
CHEESECAKE BITES

MAPLE BACON CHEESECAKE BITES

PREP 35 minutes
BAKE 10 minutes at 400°F + 25 minutes at 350°F
COOL 5 minutes
CHILL 2 hours

14 slices bacon, cut in half crosswise
½ cup all-purpose flour
2 Tbsp. ground toasted pecans
1 Tbsp. sugar
¼ cup butter
1 8-oz. pkg. cream cheese, softened
3 Tbsp. butter, softened
2 Tbsp. pure maple syrup
1 egg
¼ tsp. apple pie spice
¼ cup pure maple syrup
¼ cup chopped toasted pecans

1. Preheat oven to 400°F. Grease twenty-four 1¾-inch muffin cups. Line a 15×10-inch baking pan with foil. Arrange bacon slices in prepared pan. Bake 8 to 10 minutes or until brown but not crisp. Remove 24 of the bacon pieces; cool until easy to handle. Bake remaining bacon 2 to 4 minutes more or until crisp. Drain on paper towels; crumble. Set crumbled bacon aside. Line the sides of each prepared muffin cup with a bacon slice. Reduce oven temperature to 350°F.
2. In a bowl stir together flour, ground pecans, and sugar. Using a pastry blender, cut in the ¼ cup butter until crumbly. Sprinkle pecan mixture into each bacon-lined muffin cup; press down with fingers. Bake 10 minutes.
3. Meanwhile, for filling, in a medium bowl beat cream cheese, 3 Tbsp. butter, and maple syrup with a mixer on medium until light and fluffy. Beat in egg and apple pie spice, scraping bowl as needed. Stir in crumbled bacon.
4. Spoon filling into partially baked crusts. Bake 15 minutes more or until filling is set. Cool in muffin cups on a wire rack 5 minutes. Carefully remove from muffin cups; cool on wire rack. Cover and chill 2 hours or until firm or up to 24 hours. Before serving, drizzle with maple syrup and sprinkle with chopped pecans. Makes 24 servings.
PER SERVING *124 cal., 10 g fat (5 g sat. fat), 32 mg chol., 151 mg sodium, 7 g carb., 0 g fiber, 3 g pro.*

RUSTIC SWISS CHARD AND MOZZARELLA TART

PREP 30 minutes
BAKE 30 minutes at 400°F

1 recipe Pastry
1 bunch Swiss chard, washed and chopped (about 5 cups)
1 cup chopped leeks
4 cloves garlic, minced
¼ tsp. dried thyme, crushed
¼ tsp. salt
¼ tsp. black pepper
1 Tbsp. olive oil
¾ cup shredded mozzarella cheese
Fresh Italian parsley (optional)

1. Prepare Pastry. Wrap and refrigerate (up to 1 hour) while preparing filling.
2. Preheat oven to 400°F. For filling, in a large skillet cook chard, leeks, garlic, thyme, salt, and pepper in hot oil over medium heat 4 minutes or until chard is wilted and leeks are tender. Cool slightly. Stir in cheese; set aside.
3. On a lightly floured surface, roll pastry to a 12-inch circle. Transfer to greased baking sheet lined with parchment paper. Spoon filling into center of pastry circle, leaving a 2-inch border. Fold pastry edge over filling, pleating edges of dough. Bake 30 to 40 minutes or until golden. Sprinkle with parsley; serve warm. Makes 8 servings.
Pastry In a large bowl combine 1¼ cups all-purpose flour and ¼ tsp. salt. Cut up ½ cup cold butter; cut into flour until mixture resembles coarse meal. Combine ¼ cup ice cold water, ¼ cup sour cream, and 2 tsp. lemon juice. Add half the sour cream mixture to flour mixture; toss with a fork. Add remaining sour cream mixture; toss with fork until pastry is moistened. Form into a ball.
PER SERVING *487 cal., 34 g fat (19 g sat. fat), 79 mg chol., 709 mg sodium, 37 g carb., 2 g fiber, 11 g pro.*

RUSTIC SWISS CHARD AND MOZZARELLA TART

GARLICKY ASPARAGUS
FLATBREADS

GARLICKY ASPARAGUS FLATBREADS

PREP 20 minutes
BAKE 18 minutes at 450°F

- 1 lb. pizza dough
- 2 Tbsp. butter
- 3 large cloves garlic, minced
- 2 Tbsp. all-purpose flour
- 1 cup milk
- ½ cup finely shredded Parmesan cheese
- 6 oz. mozzarella cheese, sliced or shredded
- 1 lb. green, white, and/or purple asparagus, trimmed and cut in 3-inch lengths
- 1 medium yellow squash, sliced (about 2½ cups)
- 1 Tbsp. olive oil
   Cracked black pepper
- ¼ cup thinly sliced green onions
   Honey

1. Preheat oven to 450°F. Grease two 15×10×1-inch baking pans; set aside. For flatbreads, cut thawed dough in half. On a lightly floured surface, roll each half to a 15×10-inch rectangle. (If dough becomes difficult to roll, let rest 5 minutes, then resume rolling.) Press dough into prepared pans, pressing to sides of pans. Prick dough all over with a fork. Bake on separate oven racks 6 to 8 minutes or until very lightly browned.

2. Meanwhile, for white sauce, in a small saucepan melt the butter over medium heat; stir in garlic. Cook 30 seconds. Stir in flour. Cook and stir 2 minutes. Slowly whisk in milk. Cook and stir until thickened and bubbly. Add Parmesan cheese and stir until melted.

3. Spread white sauce over the dough to within ½ inch of edges. Top with mozzarella cheese. In a large bowl lightly toss asparagus and squash with 1 Tbsp. of olive oil. Arrange vegetables on cheese layer. Sprinkle with black pepper. Bake on separate oven racks 12 minutes or until browned, rotating pans halfway through. Cool slightly.

4. Sprinkle with green onions and drizzle with honey. Makes 24 servings.

PER SERVING *111 cal., 4 g fat (2 g sat. fat), 10 mg chol., 172 mg sodium, 14 g carb., 1 g fiber, 4 g pro.*

FETA CROSTINI WITH
TOMATO, BACON, AND
APPLE JAM

FETA CROSTINI WITH TOMATO, BACON, AND APPLE JAM

PREP 15 minutes
COOK 17 minutes
STAND 10 minutes

½ lb. smoked bacon
1 28-oz. can diced tomatoes, drained
1 cup sugar
1 medium apple, peeled, cored, and diced
1 small yellow onion, diced
3 Tbsp. cider vinegar
1 tsp. salt
¼ tsp. black pepper
1 loaf baguette-style French bread, thinly sliced and toasted (30 slices)
8 oz. feta cheese, crumbled
Snipped fresh chives

1. In an extra-large skillet over medium heat, cook bacon until browned and crisp, 5 to 8 minutes. Transfer bacon to paper towels to drain. Crumble or cut into small pieces.

2. In a large saucepan combine the drained tomatoes, sugar, apple, onion, vinegar, salt, pepper, and bacon. Bring to boiling over medium heat and cook, uncovered, 12 to 15 minutes or until apples are tender and liquid is reduced, stirring frequently.

3. Remove pan from heat; let stand 10 minutes.

4. Arrange baguette slices on a serving platter. Top with tomato, bacon, and apple jam, the feta, and chives. Makes 30 servings.

PER SERVING *116 cal., 3 g fat (2 g sat. fat), 10 mg chol., 350 mg sodium, 17 g carb., 1 g fiber, 4 g pro.*

PARMESAN HAM
AND CHEESE
TOASTS

PARMESAN HAM AND CHEESE TOASTS

START TO FINISH 25 minutes

- 2 Tbsp. butter
- 2 Tbsp. olive oil
- 1 clove garlic, minced
- 1 10-oz. loaf baguette-style French bread, cut diagonally into ¼-inch slices
- 18 Canadian-style bacon slices, cut in half
- 1½ cups shredded mozzarella cheese
- ½ cup finely shredded Parmigiano-Reggiano cheese (2 oz.)
  Peach or apricot preserves (optional)

1. Preheat oven to 400°F. In a small saucepan combine butter, oil, and garlic. Cook over medium heat until butter is melted. Remove from heat.
2. Lightly brush butter mixture lightly on both sides of bread slices. Arrange bread slices in a single layer on a large baking sheet. Bake 6 to 8 minutes or until golden. Top each slice with a half slice of Canadian bacon. Combine mozzarella and Parmigiano-Reggiano cheeses; sprinkle on bacon slices.
3. Bake toasts 5 to 6 minutes or until cheese is melted and bubbly. If desired, top warm toasts with peach preserves. Makes 36 servings.
PER SERVING *57 cal., 3 g fat (1 g sat. fat), 10 mg chol., 159 mg sodium, 4 g carb., 0 g fiber, 4 g pro.*

ROASTED PEPPER QUESO FUNDIDO

PREP 35 minutes
ROAST 20 minutes at 425°F
STAND 15 minutes

- 2 fresh poblano chile peppers (tip, page 29)
- 1 small red sweet pepper
- 3 cups shredded Monterey Jack cheese with jalapeño peppers (12 oz.)
- 2 Tbsp. all-purpose flour
- ⅓ cup finely chopped onion
- 1 Tbsp. butter
- ½ tsp. ground cumin
- ¾ cup half-and-half
  Tortilla chips

ROASTED PEPPER QUESO FUNDIDO

1. Preheat oven to 425°F. Quarter poblano peppers and sweet pepper lengthwise; remove stems, seeds, and membranes. Place pepper pieces, cut sides down, on a foil-lined baking sheet. Bake 20 to 25 minutes or until skins are blistered and dark. Bring foil up around peppers to enclose. Let stand 15 minutes or until cool. Using a sharp knife, loosen edges of skins; gently pull off skin in strips and discard. Finely chop peppers.
2. In a large bowl stir together cheeses and flour; set aside. In a medium saucepan cook onion in hot butter over medium heat until tender. Add cumin; cook and stir 1 minute. Stir in half-and-half.
3. Gradually add cheese mixture, stirring constantly over low heat until cheese is melted. Stir in roasted peppers. If necessary, stir in additional half-and-half to make dip desired consistency. Serve with chips. Makes 12 servings.
PER SERVING *158 cal., 12 g fat (8 g sat. fat), 38 mg chol., 205 mg sodium, 5 g carb., 0 g fiber, 8 g pro.*

SMOKY BLUE CHEESE DIP

START TO FINISH 10 minutes

- 1 clove garlic, peeled
- ¼ tsp. kosher salt
- 2 tsp. white wine vinegar or champagne vinegar
- 1 6-oz. container plain Greek yogurt
- ¼ cup mayonnaise
- ½ tsp. smoked paprika
- ⅛ tsp. freshly ground black pepper
- 8 oz. blue cheese, crumbled (2 cups)

1. Place garlic on a cutting board; sprinkle with salt. Using the side of a chef's knife, smear garlic and salt together to form a paste. Transfer to a medium bowl. Whisk in vinegar. Stir in yogurt, mayonnaise, smoked paprika, and pepper. Fold in blue cheese. Makes 16 servings.
PER SERVING *84 cal., 7 g fat (3 g sat. fat), 13 mg chol., 254 mg sodium, 1 g carb., 0 g fiber, 4 g pro.*

PEAR SPARKLER

START TO FINISH 30 minutes

    Ice
6   Tbsp. pear nectar
1   Tbsp. Rosemary Syrup
¼   to ⅓ cup ginger ale, chilled
    Fresh rosemary sprig (optional)

1. Fill a tall narrow glass with ice. Add pear nectar and Rosemary Syrup. Slowly pour in ginger ale; stir gently to combine. If desired, serve with a rosemary sprig. Makes 1 servings.

Rosemary Syrup In a small saucepan combine ½ cup sugar, ½ cup water, and 3 sprigs fresh rosemary. Bring to boiling, stirring to dissolve sugar; reduce heat. Simmer, uncovered, 10 minutes or until syrupy. Remove from heat; cool completely. Strain the syrup.

PER SERVING *127 cal., 0 g fat, 0 mg chol., 9 mg sodium, 33 g carb., 1 g fiber, 0 g pro.*

SPICED HOT BUTTERED RUM

SPICED HOT BUTTERED RUM

PREP 15 minutes
SLOW COOK 7 hours (low) or 3½ hours (high)

3   1-inch strips lemon zest
1   3-inch stick cinnamon
1   tsp. whole cloves
4   cups cranberry-raspberry juice blend
2   cups apple cider or apple juice
2   cups water
½   cup sugar
¼   cup lemon juice
1   cup rum or bourbon (optional)
    Butter
    Cinnamon sticks (optional)

1. For spice bag, cut a 6-inch square from a double thickness of 100%-cotton cheesecloth. Place lemon peel, the 3-inch stick cinnamon, and the cloves in the center of the cheesecloth. Bring corners together; tie closed with 100%-cotton kitchen string.

2. In a 3½- to 5-quart slow cooker combine spice bag, cranberry-raspberry juice blend, apple cider, the water, sugar, and lemon juice. Stir to dissolve sugar. Cover and cook on low 7 to 8 hours or high 3½ to 4 hours. Discard spice bag. If desired, stir in rum. Serve immediately or keep warm, covered, on warm or low setting up to 2 hours.

3. Ladle into mugs or cups. Float about ½ teaspoon butter on each serving. If desired, add a cinnamon stick to each mug. Makes 8 servings.

To Make Ahead Prepare spice bag as directed in Step 1. Place in an airtight container; cover. Store in the refrigerator up to 3 days.

PER SERVING *162 cal., 2 g fat (1 g sat. fat), 5 mg chol., 26 mg sodium, 32 g carb.*

WINTER CRANBERRY SIPPER

PREP 10 minutes
STAND 24 hours

    Ice
6   Tbsp. cranberry juice
3   Tbsp. Infused Vanilla Vodka or purchased vanilla vodka
3   Tbsp. ginger ale, chilled

1. Fill a cocktail shaker with ice. In the cocktail shaker combine cranberry juice and Infused Vanilla Vodka. Cover and shake 10 seconds or until cold.

2. Fill a chilled tall glass with ice; strain vodka mixture into glass. Slowly pour in ginger ale; stir gently to combine. Makes 1 serving.

Infused Vanilla Vodka Slice 1 vanilla bean in half lengthwise. Add to a 750-ml. bottle of vodka; stand in a dark place for 1 to 2 days. Strain vanilla bean from vodka and return vodka to bottle.

PER SERVING *163 cal., 0 g fat, 0 g chol., 6 mg sodium, 17 g carb, 0 g fiber, 0 g pro.*

HOT COFFEE LATTE EGGNOG

START TO FINISH 30 minutes

3   eggs, slightly beaten
2   cups whole milk
1   cup heavy cream
½   cup coffee liqueur
2   Tbsp. honey
1   Tbsp. instant espresso powder or 4 tsp. instant coffee crystals
    Whipped cream (optional)
    Ground cinnamon
8   long cinnamon sticks (optional)

1. In a large heavy saucepan stir together eggs, milk, cream, coffee liqueur, honey, and espresso powder. Cook and stir over medium heat 20 minutes or just until mixture coats a metal spoon and thermometer registers 170°F; do not boil.

2. Top hot eggnog with whipped cream, if desired, and sprinkle with ground cinnamon. Serve with cinnamon sticks, if desired. Makes 8 servings.

PER SERVING *239 cal., 15 g fat (9 g sat. fat), 127 mg chol., 64 mg sodium, 14 g carb., 0 g fiber, 5 g pro.*

Nonalcoholic Coffee Latte Eggnog: Prepare as above, except omit the coffee liqueur. Increase the milk to 2½ cups.

HOT COFFEE
LATTE EGGNOG

SOUR CREAM–
CRANBERRY MUFFINS,
PAGE 52

Weekend Brunch

Rise and shine to the smell of something wonderful baking in the oven. For Christmas morning or any day you can enjoy a leisurely wake-up, these breakfast and brunch dishes—tender muffins, flaky homemade pastries, and frittatas, fruit-topped whole-grain pancakes—are a lovely way to start the day.

CORNMEAL-SAGE
BISCUITS WITH
SAUSAGE GRAVY

CORNMEAL-SAGE BISCUITS WITH SAUSAGE GRAVY

PREP 30 minutes
BAKE 12 minutes at 450°F

- 2⅔ cups all-purpose flour
- ⅓ cup cornmeal
- 4 tsp. baking powder
- 1 Tbsp. sugar
- ¾ tsp. cream of tartar
- ½ tsp. salt
- 2 Tbsp. finely chopped green onion
- 1 tsp. finely snipped fresh sage or ¼ tsp. dried sage, crushed
- ¾ cup butter
- 1¼ cups buttermilk or sour milk*
- 1 recipe Sausage Gravy
  Chopped green onions (optional)

1. Preheat oven to 450°F. In a large bowl stir together flour, cornmeal, baking powder, sugar, cream of tartar, and salt. Stir in 2 Tbsp. green onion and sage. Using a pastry blender, cut in butter until mixture resembles coarse crumbs. Make a well in center of flour mixture. Add buttermilk all at once. Using a fork, stir just until moistened.

2. Turn out dough onto a lightly floured surface. Knead dough by folding and gently pressing just until dough holds together. Pat or lightly roll dough to ¾-inch thickness. Cut dough with a floured 2½-inch round cutter. Dip cutter into flour between cuts and reroll scraps as necessary.

3. Place dough rounds 1 inch apart on an ungreased baking sheet. Bake 12 to 14 minutes or until golden brown. Remove biscuits from baking sheet; cool slightly on wire rack.

4. Spoon Sausage Gravy over split biscuits. If desired, top with additional green onions. Makes 12 servings.

Sausage Gravy In an extra-large skillet cook 1½ pounds bulk pork sausage and 1 cup chopped onion over medium-high heat until meat is brown and onion is tender. Do not drain. Sprinkle ¼ cup all-purpose flour over meat mixture; stir to combine. Cook and stir over medium heat for 1 minute. Gradually stir in 3 cups milk. Cook and stir until thickened and bubbly. Cook and stir 1 minute more. Season to taste with salt and black pepper. If desired, stir in 2 tsp. snipped fresh thyme.

*Tip For 1¼ cups sour milk, place 4 tsp. lemon juice or vinegar in a glass measuring cup. Add milk to equal 1¼ cups liquid; stir. Let stand 5 minutes.

PER SERVING *450 cal., 28 g fat (13 g sat. fat), 77 mg chol., 714 mg sodium, 33 g carb., 1 g fiber, 15 g pro.*

POACHED CHICKEN AND AVOCADO BRUNCH BURRITOS

PREP 50 minutes
BAKE 15 minutes at 350°F

- 3 cups reduced-sodium chicken broth, divided
- ¾ cup quinoa, rinsed and drained
- 1 cup salsa verde, divided
- 12 oz. skinless boneless chicken breasts
- 2 tsp. fajita seasoning
- 6 eggs
- 3 Tbsp. fat-free milk
- ¼ tsp. garlic salt
  Nonstick cooking spray
- 1 ripe avocado, halved, seeded, peeled, and chopped
- 1 Tbsp. chopped fresh cilantro
- 8 10-inch whole wheat tortillas or flour tortillas
- 1 cup shredded reduced-fat pepper-Jack cheese or reduced-fat Mexican-style four-cheese blend (4 oz.)

1. In a small saucepan combine 1⅓ cups of the chicken broth and the quinoa. Bring to a boil; reduce heat to medium-low. Cook, covered, 10 to 15 minutes or until broth is absorbed. Remove from heat. Stir in ¼ cup of the salsa verde; set aside.

2. Meanwhile, in a medium saucepan, bring remaining 1⅔ cups chicken broth to a boil. Add chicken; return to a boil. Reduce heat and simmer, covered, 12 to 15 minutes or until chicken is done (165°F). Using a slotted spoon, transfer chicken to a cutting board; let stand until cool enough to handle. Using two forks, pull chicken into bite-size shreds; toss with fajita seasoning and set aside. Discard cooking liquid.

3. In a bowl whisk eggs. Whisk in milk and garlic salt. Coat a large nonstick skillet with cooking spray; heat skillet over medium heat. Pour egg mixture into hot skillet. As eggs begin to set, fold mixture over on itself, continuing to fold until cooked.

4. Preheat oven to 350°F. In a bowl combine avocado, ¼ cup of the salsa verde, and the cilantro. Heat tortillas according to package directions. For each burrito, spoon about 1 Tbsp. avocado mixture on one tortilla. Top with 3 Tbsp. quinoa mixture, some of the egg, shredded cheese, and shredded chicken. Fold in sides of tortilla then roll up. Place on a large baking pan, folded edges down. Spray with nonstick cooking spray.

5. Bake 15 to 20 minutes or until heated through and lightly browned on top. Top with remaining ½ cup salsa verde. Makes 8 servings.

PER SERVING *457 cal., 17 g fat (5 g sat. fat), 182 mg chol., 1,109 mg sodium, 46 g carb., 24 g fiber, 28 g pro.*

HONEY-SAGE SWEET POTATOES AND PEARS WITH WALNUTS

PREP 15 minutes
ROAST 20 minutes at 425°F

2   sweet potatoes, peeled, halved lengthwise, and sliced ½ inch thick
2   medium pears, cored and sliced ¼ inch thick
1   red onion, cut into ½-inch wedges
4   tsp. olive oil
½   tsp. kosher salt
¼   tsp. black pepper
½   cup walnuts, coarsely chopped
1   Tbsp. honey
2   tsp. chopped fresh sage

1. Preheat oven to 425°F. In a 15×10×1-inch baking pan, toss together sweet potatoes, pears, and red onion. Drizzle with olive oil and sprinkle with salt and pepper. Toss to combine. Spread in an even layer.
2. Roast 15 minutes. Stir in walnuts; roast 5 to 10 minutes or until sweet potatoes and pears are tender. Drizzle with honey and sprinkle with fresh sage. Makes 4 servings.
PER SERVING *300 cal., 15 g fat (2 g sat. fat), 305 mg sodium, 42 g carb., 7 g fiber, 4 g pro.*

HONEY-SAGE SWEET POTATOES AND PEARS WITH WALNUTS

POTATO-THYME FRITTATA

PREP 15 minutes
COOK 15 minutes
BAKE 6 minutes at 350°F
STAND 10 minutes

8   eggs
¼   cup milk
1   Tbsp. snipped fresh thyme or ½ to 1 tsp. dried thyme, crushed
½   tsp. salt, divided
¼   tsp. black pepper
2   medium potatoes peeled, if desired
2   Tbsp. butter
½   cup finely chopped onion
2   cloves garlic, minced

1. Preheat oven to 350°F. In a medium bowl beat together eggs, milk, thyme, ¼ tsp. of the salt, and the pepper. Set aside.
2. Slice potatoes in half lengthwise. Cut each halve crosswise into thin half-circle slices (2 cups).
3. In a medium cast-iron skillet or large ovenproof skillet, melt butter over medium heat. Add onion, garlic, and remaining ¼ tsp. salt. Cook, uncovered, 2 minutes, stirring occasionally. Add potatoes. Cook 7 to 10 minutes or just until potatoes are tender and starting to brown, stirring occasionally. Spread potatoes evenly in skillet.
4. Pour egg mixture over potatoes. Cook over medium heat. As eggs set, run a spatula around edge of skillet, lifting eggs so uncooked portion flows underneath. Cook and lift edges until eggs are almost set, 6 to 8 minutes total (surface will be moist).
5. Place skillet in oven and bake, uncovered, 6 to 8 minutes or just until top is set. Let stand 10 minutes before serving. If desired, sprinkle with additional thyme. Makes 6 servings.
PER SERVING *174 cal., 10 g fat (5 g sat. fat), 259 mg chol., 325 mg sodium, 10 g carb., 1 g fiber, 10 g pro.*

POTATO-THYME FRITTATA

SPICY CREAMED
CORN WITH
GREEN CHILES

SPICY CREAMED CORN WITH GREEN CHILES

PREP 20 minutes
SLOW COOK 3 hours 10 minutes (low)

- 3 16-oz. pkg. frozen whole kernel corn
- 2 7-oz. cans mild fire-roasted whole green chile peppers, drained and chopped
- 1 8-oz. tub cream cheese spread with jalapeño
- 4 oz. plain cream cheese, softened, or cream cheese spread
- 1 cup chopped onion
- 2 Tbsp. sugar
- 4 cloves garlic, minced
- 1½ tsp. salt
- ¾ tsp. black pepper
- 2 cups shredded Chihuahua cheese (8 oz.)
- 2 Tbsp. red wine vinegar
- 1 Tbsp. olive oil
- 2 tsp. sugar
- 2½ cups halved cherry tomatoes
- 3 Tbsp. snipped fresh cilantro

1. In a 5-quart slow cooker combine the first six ingredients (through 2 Tbsp. sugar), 3 of the garlic cloves, 1 tsp. of the salt, and ½ tsp. of the black pepper.
2. Cover and cook on low 3 to 3½ hours or until heated through, stirring once. Stir in Chihuahua cheese until combined. Cover and cook on low 10 minutes more. Stir to combine.
3. Meanwhile, for tomato relish, in a bowl combine vinegar, oil, 2 tsp. sugar, remaining 1 clove garlic, ½ tsp. salt, and ¼ tsp. black pepper. Stir in tomatoes and cilantro.
4. Top creamed corn with tomato relish and, if desired, additional cilantro leaves. Makes 12 servings.
PER SERVING *312 cal., 17 g fat (9 g sat. fat), 51 mg chol., 646 mg sodium, 33 g carb., 4 g fiber, 10 g pro.*

BLOOD ORANGE AND SPINACH SALAD WITH GINGER-SPICED WALNUTS

PREP 15 minutes
STAND 10 minutes
COOK 3 minutes

- 2 Tbsp. finely chopped shallot
- 2 Tbsp. champagne vinegar or white wine vinegar
- ½ tsp. Dijon mustard
- ½ tsp. blood orange or navel orange zest
- ⅛ tsp. salt
   Dash black pepper
- 2 Tbsp. olive oil
- 1 Tbsp. butter
- ½ cup walnuts, coarsely chopped
- 1 tsp. sugar
- ¼ tsp. salt
- ¼ tsp. ground ginger
   Dash cayenne pepper
- 4 cups fresh baby spinach
- 2 medium blood oranges and/or navel oranges, peeled, seeded, and sectioned

1. For dressing, in a bowl combine shallot and vinegar. Let stand 10 minutes, stirring occasionally. Stir in mustard, orange zest, salt, and pepper. Slowly whisk in olive oil.
2. For the ginger-spiced walnuts, in a small nonstick skillet, melt the butter. Add walnuts, sugar, salt, ginger, and cayenne pepper. Toss to coat. Cook over medium heat 3 to 4 minutes or until walnuts are just toasted, stirring occasionally. Remove from heat and cool walnuts completely.
3. Place spinach in a bowl; top with orange sections and cooled walnuts. Whisk dressing and drizzle over salad. Makes 6 servings.
PER SERVING *157 cal., 13 g fat (3 g sat. fat), 5 mg chol., 202 mg sodium, 14 g carb., 3 g fiber, 3 g pro.*

FRESH FRUIT WITH CITRUS MINT DRESSING

START TO FINISH 30 minutes

- ¼ cup orange juice
- 1 Tbsp. chopped fresh mint or 1 tsp. dried mint, crushed
- 1 Tbsp. honey
- 4 cups assorted citrus fruit sections and/or crosswise slices (such as blood oranges, tangelos, grapefruit, and/or navel oranges)

1. For dressing, in a medium bowl whisk together orange juice, mint, and 1 Tbsp. honey. Add fruit to dressing; toss lightly to coat. Drizzle with additional honey, if desired. Serve immediately or cover and chill up to 4 hours, stirring occasionally. Makes 6 servings.
PER SERVING *72 cal., 0 g fat, 0 mg chol., 1 mg sodium, 18 g carb., 3 g fiber, 1 g pro.*

BLOOD ORANGE AND SPINACH SALAD WITH GINGER-SPICED WALNUTS

VERY CHERRY HAZELNUT COFFEE CAKE

WHOLE-GRAIN BUTTERMILK PANCAKES

PREP 10 minutes
STAND 10 minutes
COOK 4 minutes

1½	cups white whole wheat flour
2	tsp. baking powder
¼	tsp. baking soda
¼	tsp. salt
1	large egg
1½	cups buttermilk or sour milk*
2	Tbsp. canola oil
1	Tbsp. sugar
1	tsp. vanilla
1	recipe Lemony Blackberry Sauce and Goat Cheese or Chocolate-Orange Sauce and Whipped Cream (optional)

1. In a large bowl whisk together flour, baking powder, baking soda, and salt. In another bowl whisk together egg, buttermilk, oil, sugar, and vanilla. Make a well in center of flour mixture; add egg mixture and whisk just until combined. (Do not overmix.) Let batter stand, without stirring, 10 to 15 minutes.
2. Coat a large nonstick skillet with cooking spray; heat over medium heat. Without stirring batter, measure about ¼ cup batter for each pancake and pour onto skillet. Cook 2 to 4 minutes on each side or until golden brown; turn when surfaces are bubbly and edges are slightly dry. If desired, serve with one or both sauces (below). Makes 6 servings.
* For sour milk, combine 1 Tbsp. lemon juice or vinegar and enough milk to equal 1 cup; let stand 10 minutes.
PER SERVING *187 cal., 6 g fat (1 g sat. fat), 33 mg chol., 388 mg sodium, 28 g carb., 3 g fiber, 7 g pro.*

Lemony Blackberry Sauce and Goat Cheese In a small saucepan heat blackberry syrup and fresh or frozen blackberries over low heat until syrup is warm and berries are slightly softened. Sprinkle with goat cheese (chèvre) and lemon zest.

Chocolate-Orange Sauce and Whipped Cream In a small saucepan heat orange marmalade over low heat, stirring until smooth and warm. Spoon over pancakes; top with semisweet chocolate pieces, whipped cream, and orange zest.

VERY CHERRY HAZELNUT COFFEE CAKE

PREP 35 minutes
STAND 10 minutes
RISE 1 hour
BAKE 18 minutes at 350°F
COOL 10 minutes

⅔	cup warm milk (105°F to 115°F)
1	pkg. active dry yeast
⅓	cup unsalted butter, softened
¼	cup sugar
2	eggs, separated
1	tsp. lemon zest
½	tsp. salt
2	cups all-purpose flour
½	cup cherry preserves
2	Tbsp. unsalted butter
1	Tbsp. fresh lemon juice
1	cup fresh or frozen unsweetened pitted tart red cherries, thawed and drained
¼	cup all-purpose flour
¼	cup sugar
¼	tsp. ground ginger
¼	tsp. ground cinnamon
3	Tbsp. salted butter
½	cup chopped hazelnuts

1. In a bowl combine milk and yeast. Let stand 10 minutes.
2. In a large bowl beat together ⅓ cup unsalted butter and ¼ cup sugar with a mixer on medium until smooth. Add egg yolks, lemon zest and salt; beat until smooth. Beat in yeast mixture. Beat in 2 cups flour just until blended.
3. Thoroughly wash beaters. In a medium bowl beat egg whites until frothy; beat into dough. Spread dough into a greased 15×10×1-inch baking pan.
4. Cover and let rise in a warm place 1 hour or until doubled in size. In a small saucepan combine cherry preserves, 2 Tbsp. unsalted butter, and lemon juice. Stir over low heat until butter is melted and mixture is smooth. Let cool. Scatter cherries over dough; drizzle cooled preserve mixture over cherries.
5. Preheat oven to 350°F. For crumb topping, in a bowl combine ¼ cup flour, ¼ cup sugar, ginger, and cinnamon. Using a pastry blender or fork, cut in 3 Tbsp. butter until pieces are pea size. Stir in nuts. Sprinkle on cake. Bake 18 to 23 minutes or until lightly browned. Cool 10 minutes Makes 16 servings.
PER SERVING *226 cal., 11 g fat (5 g sat. fat), 44 mg chol., 110 mg sodium, 29 g carb., 1 g fiber, 4 g pro.*

WHOLE-GRAIN BUTTERMILK PANCAKES
WITH LEMONY BLACKBERRY SAUCE
AND GOAT CHEESE

CHRISTMAS ROLLS

PREP 45 minutes
RISE 1 hour 15 minutes
REST 10 minutes
BAKE 30 minutes at 350°F
COOL 10 minutes

- 4 to 4½ cups all-purpose flour
- 1 pkg. active dry yeast
- 1 cup milk
- 1 cup mashed potato (instant or homemade)
- ⅓ cup butter, cut up
- ⅓ cup granulated sugar
- 1 tsp. salt
- 2 eggs
- ½ cup butter, softened
- ⅓ cup cherry preserves
- 1½ cups fresh or frozen cranberries
- 1 recipe Cinnamon Roll Icing

1. In a large bowl combine 1½ cups of the flour and the yeast; set aside. In a medium saucepan heat and stir milk, mashed potato, the ⅓ cup butter, granulated sugar, and salt just until warm (120°F to 130°F) and butter is almost melted; add to flour mixture along with eggs. Beat with a mixer on low to medium 30 seconds, scraping sides of bowl constantly. Beat on high 3 minutes. Stir in as much of the remaining flour as you can.

2. Turn out dough onto a lightly floured surface. Knead in enough of the remaining flour to make a moderately soft dough that is smooth and elastic (3 to 5 minutes total kneading time). Shape dough into a ball. Place in a lightly greased bowl; turn once. Cover; let rise in a warm place until double in size (45 to 60 minutes).

3. Punch down dough. Turn out dough onto a lightly floured surface. Cover and let rest 10 minutes. Meanwhile, lightly grease a 13×9-inch baking dish or pan.

4. Roll dough into an 18×12-inch rectangle. Spread the ½ cup butter on dough. Spread cherry preserves on butter, leaving 1 inch unfilled along one long side. Top with cranberries. Roll into a spiral, starting from long side with filling. Pinch dough to seal seams.

CHRISTMAS ROLLS

5. Cut spiral into 12 equal pieces. Arrange pieces, cut sides down, in prepared baking dish. Cover with a clean kitchen towel and let stand in a warm place until nearly double in size (about 30 minutes).
6. Preheat oven to 350°F. Bake 30 to 35 minutes or until golden brown and done in center (200°F). Cool in dish on wire rack 10 minutes. Remove from dish, if desired. Drizzle or spread with Cinnamon Roll Icing. Serve warm. Makes 12 servings.
Cinnamon Roll Icing In a bowl stir together 3 cups powdered sugar, 1 tsp. vanilla, and enough milk to reach thick drizzling consistency (4 to 5 Tbsp.).
PER SERVING *473 cal., 15 g fat (9 g sat. fat), 67 mg chol., 325 mg sodium, 79 g carb., 2 g fiber, 7 g pro.*

RUBY-RED BREAKFAST TURNOVERS

PREP 30 minutes
BAKE 14 minutes at 400°F
STAND 5 minutes

1½ cups coarsely shredded, peeled red beets
1   Tbsp. butter
1   medium red cooking apple, (such as Jonathan or Rome), cored and coarsely shredded
¼   cup honey
½   tsp. apple pie spice
½   17.3-oz. pkg. frozen puff pastry, thawed (1 sheet)
1   egg white
1   Tbsp. water
    Coarse sugar

1. Preheat oven to 400°F. In a medium skillet cook shredded beets in hot butter over medium heat 4 minutes, stirring occasionally. Add apple; cook 2 to 3 minutes more or just until beets and apple are tender, stirring occasionally. Remove skillet from heat; stir in honey and apple pie spice. Cool slightly.
2. Line a baking sheet with parchment paper; set aside. Unfold puff pastry sheet on a lightly floured surface. Using a rolling pin, roll pastry to a 12-inch square. Cut into four 6-inch squares.
3. Spoon one-fourth of the filling into the center of each pastry square. Fold each square in half diagonally to make a triangle. Using a fork, press edges

RUBY-RED BREAKFAST TURNOVERS

together to seal. Transfer turnovers to prepared baking sheet.
4. In a small bowl lightly beat the egg white and the water until foamy. Brush egg wash onto turnovers. Using a sharp knife, cut a few slits in each turnover. Sprinkle lightly with coarse sugar.

5. Bake 14 to 16 minutes or until pastry is puffed and golden brown. Transfer turnovers to a wire rack. Let stand 5 minutes before serving. Serve warm. Makes 4 servings.
PER SERVING *486 cal., 26 g fat (8 g sat. fat), 7 mg chol., 233 mg sodium, 59 g carb., 4 g fiber, 6 g pro.*

CHERRY-POMEGRANATE DANISH

PREP 25 minutes
BAKE 15 minutes at 400°F

2 cups frozen unsweetened pitted dark sweet cherries
½ cup granulated sugar
½ cup pomegranate juice
3 Tbsp. cornstarch
1 tsp. vanilla
1 egg
1 Tbsp. water
1 17.3-oz. pkg. frozen puff pastry sheets (2 sheets), thawed
1 cup powdered sugar
3 oz. cream cheese, softened
2 Tbsp. milk
½ tsp. vanilla

1. Preheat oven to 400°F. Line two large baking sheets with parchment paper; set aside. In a medium saucepan combine the cherries, sugar, ½ cup pomegranate juice, cornstarch, and vanilla. Cook and stir over medium heat until thickened and bubbly. Cook and stir 2 minutes more. Remove from heat; cool slightly.
2. For the egg wash, in a small bowl combine egg and the water.
3. Unfold pastry. Cut each pastry sheet into 12 squares. Spoon a rounded tablespoon of filling in center of half of the squares, leaving a ½-inch border along edges. Using a small pastry brush, brush edges of pastry with egg wash. Place remaining pastry squares over filling. Using tines of a fork, gently press (or crimp) edges together to form a tight seal. Prick tops of danishes several times with a fork. Place 2 inches apart on prepared baking sheets. Brush tops with remaining egg wash.
4. Bake 15 to 18 minutes or until puffed and golden brown. Cool slightly on baking sheet on wire rack.
5. Meanwhile, in a small bowl stir together powdered sugar and cream cheese. Add enough of the 2 Tbsp. milk and vanilla for drizzling consistency. Drizzle over danishes. Makes 12 servings.
PER SERVING *358 cal., 18 g fat (5 g sat. fat), 23 mg chol., 136 mg sodium, 44 g carb., 1 g fiber, 4 g pro.*

SOUR CREAM-CRANBERRY MUFFINS

PREP 30 minutes
BAKE 20 minutes at 350°F
COOL 10 minutes

Nonstick cooking spray
1½ cups all-purpose flour
2 tsp. baking powder
¼ tsp. baking soda
¼ tsp. salt
¼ cup butter
1 8-oz. carton sour cream or plain yogurt
½ cup granulated sugar
½ cup milk
1 egg, lightly beaten
¾ cup dried cranberries
¼ cup packed brown sugar
¼ cup chopped pecans
2 Tbsp. granulated sugar
1 tsp. pumpkin pie spice

1. Preheat oven to 350°F. Lightly coat twelve 2½-inch muffins cups with cooking spray.
2. In a large bowl stir together flour, baking powder, baking soda, and salt. Cut in butter until mixture is crumbly.
3. In a bowl stir together sour cream, ½ cup sugar, milk, and egg. Add to flour mixture and stir just until combined. Fold in dried cranberries.
4. Stir together brown sugar, pecans, 2 Tbsp. granulated sugar, and pumpkin pie spice.
5. Spoon half the batter into prepared muffin cups. Sprinkle half of the nut mixture on batter in cups. Top with remaining batter and remaining nut mixture.
6. Bake 20 to 25 minutes or until a toothpick inserted in centers comes out clean. Cool 10 minutes in pan on wire rack. Serve warm. Makes 12 servings.
PER SERVING *234 cal., 10 g fat (5 g sat. fat), 37 mg chol., 165 mg sodium, 33 g carb., 1 g fiber, 3 g pro.*

CHERRY POMEGRANATE DANISH

SOUR CREAM-
CRANBERRY
MUFFINS

BLUEBERRY SWIRLY
SMOOTHIES

STRAWBERRY SHORTCAKE SCONES

PREP 20 minutes
BAKE 16 minutes at 400°F

1   cup chopped fresh strawberries
2½ cups plus 1 Tbsp. all-purpose flour
3   Tbsp. granulated sugar
1   Tbsp. baking powder
¼   tsp. salt
6   Tbsp. butter
1   egg, lightly beaten
¾   cup whole milk ricotta cheese
¼   cup heavy cream
      Heavy cream
      Coarse sugar

1. Preheat oven to 400°F. In a bowl toss together strawberries and 1 Tbsp. flour. In a large bowl combine 2½ cups flour, 3 Tbsp. sugar, baking powder, and salt. Using a pastry blender, cut in butter until mixture resembles coarse crumbs. Make a well in center of flour mixture.
2. In a medium bowl combine egg, ricotta, and heavy cream. Add all at once to flour mixture. Add strawberries. Using a fork, stir just until moistened.
3. Turn dough out onto a lightly floured surface. Knead dough by folding and gently pressing 10 to 12 strokes or until dough is nearly smooth. Pat into a 10×4-inch rectangle. Cut in half lengthwise and in sixths crosswise to make 12 rectangles.
4. Place rectangles 2 inches apart on a parchment paper-lined baking sheet. Brush with additional heavy cream. Sprinkle with coarse sugar. Bake 16 minutes or until golden brown. Serve warm. Makes 12 servings.
PER SERVING *227 cal., 11 g fat (7 g sat. fat), 49 mg chol., 238 mg sodium, 27 g carb., 1 g fiber, 5 g pro.*

BLUEBERRY SWIRLY SMOOTHIES

START TO FINISH 10 minutes

2   cups frozen blueberries
½   cup apple juice
1   6-oz. carton plain fat-free yogurt
1   ripe banana, peeled, cut up, and frozen
2   to 3 tsp. honey

STRAWBERRY SHORTCAKE SCONES

1. In a blender combine blueberries and juice. Cover and blend until smooth. Divide among three glasses. Wash blender.
2. In the blender combine yogurt, banana, and honey. Cover and blend until smooth. Spoon over smoothie in glasses. Swirl with a spoon. Makes 3 servings.
PER SERVING *148 cal., 1 g fat, 1 mg chol., 41 mg sodium, 34 g carb., 4 g fiber, 4 g pro.*

WHITE HOT CHOCOLATE

START TO FINISH 20 minutes

3   oz. white baking chocolate with cocoa butter, chopped
2   cups milk or half-and-half
⅓   cup hot strong coffee
½   tsp. vanilla
      Grated nutmeg (optional)
      Grated dark and/or white chocolate (optional)

1. In a medium saucepan combine white chocolate and ⅓ cup of the milk. Stir over low heat until chocolate is melted. Add remaining milk. Stir until heated through. Add coffee and vanilla. If desired, top servings with nutmeg and/or grated chocolate. Makes 4 servings.
PER SERVING *184 cal., 9 g fat (6 g sat. fat), 14 mg chol., 73 mg sodium, 18 g carb., 0 g fiber, 6 g pro.*

CHAI TEA BASE

PREP 15 minutes
SLOW COOK 6 hours (low) or 3 hours (high)
STAND 10 minutes

8   cups water
⅔   cup honey
4   2- to 3-inch sticks cinnamon
2   inches fresh ginger, thinly sliced
½   tsp. whole cardamom seeds (without pods)
16 whole cloves
16 whole black peppercorns
¼   tsp. ground nutmeg
12 black tea bags
7   cups low-fat milk

1. In a 3½- or 4-quart slow cooker stir together the water and honey until dissolved. Add stick cinnamon, ginger, cardamom seeds, cloves, peppercorns, and nutmeg.
2. Cover and cook 6 to 8 hours on low or 3 to 4 hours on high. Add tea bags. Cover; let stand 10 minutes. Strain through a fine-mesh sieve lined with a double thickness of 100%-cotton cheesecloth. Refrigerate up to 2 weeks.
3. For each serving, use ½ cup Chai Tea Base and ½ cup low-fat milk. Heat to steaming. Makes 14 servings.
PER SERVING *104 cal., 1 g fat (1 g sat. fat), 6 mg chol., 59 mg sodium, 20 g carb., 0 g fiber, 4 g pro.*

From-Scratch Breads

The simple combination of water, flour, and leavening yields a dizzying variety of results—from crisp-crusted, chewy yeast breads to soft and buttery breakfast braids to tender-crumbed quick breads and muffins. At the time of year when you want your home to be as warm and welcoming as possible, the smell of fresh bread baking in the oven is the perfect answer.

EVERYDAY ARTISAN
BREAD, PAGE 59

CARDAMOM
BRAID

CARDAMOM BRAID

PREP 20 minutes
REST 20 minutes
RISE 2 hours
BAKE 25 minutes at 375°F

1   package active dry yeast
1   tsp. sugar
¼   cup warm water (105°F to 115°F)
¾   cup warm milk (105°F to 115°F)
½   cup sugar
¼   cup butter, melted and cooled
2   Tbsp. vegetable oil
1   Tbsp. orange zest
¾   tsp. ground cardamom
½   tsp. salt
3½ to 4 cups all-purpose flour
    Coarse granulated sugar

1. In a small bowl dissolve yeast and 1 tsp. sugar in the warm water; let stand 10 minutes.

2. In a large bowl combine warm milk, ½ cup sugar, melted and cooled butter, oil, orange zest, cardamom, and salt. Beat with a mixer on low to medium until combined. Stir in 1 cup of the flour. Add the yeast mixture. Beat with a mixer on low to medium 30 seconds, scraping bowl constantly. Beat on high 3 minutes. One cup at a time, stir in 2 cups flour. (Dough should be slightly wet.) Cover; let dough rest 10 minutes.

3. Turn out dough onto a lightly floured surface. Knead in enough remaining flour to make a moderately soft dough that is smooth and elastic (3 to 5 minutes total). Shape dough into a ball. Place in a lightly greased bowl, turning once to grease surface. Cover; let rise in a warm place until doubled in size (1 to 1¼ hours).

4. Punch down dough. Turn out dough onto a lightly floured surface. Cover; let rest 10 minutes.

5. Divide dough into thirds. Shape each portion into a 14-inch-long rope. Place ropes 1 inch apart on a lightly greased baking sheet. Starting at center, loosely braid to each end. Pinch ends to seal and tuck under loaf. Cover; let rise in a warm place until nearly doubled (about 1 hour).

6. Lightly brush or mist top of braid with water; sprinkle with coarse sugar.

7. Preheat oven to 375°F. Bake 25 to 30 minutes or until bread sounds hollow when top is tapped. (Internal temperature should be 180°F.) If necessary cover loosely with foil the last 10 minutes to prevent overbrowning. Remove from baking sheet. Cool on a wire rack. Makes 1 loaf (10 slices).

PER SLICE *282 cal., 8 g fat (3 g sat. fat), 14 mg chol., 167 mg sodium, 47 g carb., 1 g fiber, 5 g pro.*

EVERYDAY ARTISAN BREAD

PREP 15 minutes
STAND 2 hours
RISE 20 minutes
BAKE 25 minutes at 450°F

3   cups all-purpose flour
3   cups whole wheat flour
¾   cup dry-roasted sunflower kernels
3   Tbsp. flaxseeds
3   Tbsp. sesame seeds
3   Tbsp. poppy seeds
4   tsp. kosher salt
1   pkg. active dry yeast
3   cups warm water (120°F to 130°F)
    Cornmeal
    All-purpose flour

1. In an extra-large bowl combine the first eight ingredients (through yeast). Add the warm water. Stir until flour mixture is moistened (dough will be very sticky and soft). Cover loosely with plastic wrap. Let stand at room temperature 2 hours. Bake as directed in Step 2 or refrigerate up to 7 days.*

2. To bake bread, grease a large cast-iron skillet or baking sheet. (Or place a baking stone on center rack of oven before preheating. Transfer loaf from prepared baking sheet to baking stone. Bake as directed.) Dust generously with cornmeal or flour. With a knife score dough in bowl into thirds. With floured hands, scoop out one-third of the dough. Do not punch dough down. Place dough portion on a well-floured surface. Lightly flour top of dough. Shape dough by gently pulling it into a ball, tucking edges under. Add more flour as needed to prevent dough from sticking to hands. Place dough in prepared skillet or on baking sheet. Sprinkle lightly with flour. Cover loosely with plastic wrap. Let rise in a warm place 20 minutes (if dough was refrigerated, let rise 45 minutes.)

3. Preheat oven to 450°F. Using a sharp knife, score bread top. Place on rack in center of oven. Place a shallow roasting pan with 2 cups hot tap water on rack below. Bake 25 to 30 minutes or until crust is deep golden brown. Transfer loaf from pan to wire rack; cool completely. Makes 3 loaves (30 slices).

* Dough becomes stickier the longer it stands in the refrigerator. Be careful to not overwork the dough so as not to destroy air pockets that formed.

PER SLICE *122 cal., 3 g fat (0 g sat. fat), 285 mg sodium, 20 g carb., 3 g fiber, 4 g pro.*

EVERYDAY ARTISAN BREAD

ENGLISH MUFFINS IN A LOAF WITH HONEY BUTTER

PREP 35 minutes
RISE 45 minutes
BAKE 25 minutes at 400°F

    Cornmeal
6   cups all-purpose flour
2   pkg. active dry yeast
¼   tsp. baking soda
2   cups milk
½   cup water
1   Tbsp. sugar
1   tsp. salt
    Cornmeal
1   recipe Honey Butter (optional)

1. Lightly grease two 8×4×2-inch loaf pans. Lightly sprinkle with cornmeal to coat bottom and sides. Set aside.
2. In a large mixing bowl combine 3 cups of the flour, the yeast, and baking soda; set aside. In a medium saucepan heat milk, the water, sugar, and salt over medium heat just until warm (120°F to 130°F), stirring occasionally. Add milk mixture to flour mixture; mix well. Stir in remaining flour.

3. Divide dough in half. Place in prepared loaf pans. Sprinkle tops with cornmeal. Cover; let rise in a warm place 45 minutes, or until double in size.
4. Preheat oven to 400°F. Bake loaves 25 minutes or until golden. Immediately remove loaves from pans. Cool on a wire rack.
5. Toast slices and serve with Honey Butter, if desired. Makes 2 loaves (32 slices).
PER SLICE *90 cal., 1 g fat (0 g sat. fat), 1 mg chol., 91 mg sodium, 18 g carb., 1 g fiber, 3 g pro.*
Honey Butter In a bowl beat ½ cup softened butter and ¼ cup honey with a mixer on low until well mixed. Store in the refrigerator.

CHEESY BACON PULL-APART BREAD

PREP 1 hour
RISE 1 hour 30 minutes
REST 10 minutes
BAKE 25 minutes at 350°F

1   cup milk
¼   cup sugar
¼   cup butter, cut up

CHEESY BACON PULL-APART BREAD

½   cup yellow cornmeal
1   tsp. salt
1   pkg. active dry yeast
¼   cup warm water (105°F to 115°F)
1   egg, lightly beaten
3½   to 4 cups all-purpose flour
20   ¾-inch cubes Monterey Jack cheese with jalapeño peppers (5 oz.)
4   slices bacon, crisp-cooked and crumbled (¼ cup)
¼   cup thinly sliced green onion
¼   cup butter, melted
¼   yellow cornmeal
¼   cup grated Parmesan cheese
     Nacho cheese dip, warmed (optional)

1. In small saucepan heat and stir the first five ingredients (through salt) just until warm (105°F to 115°F) and butter is almost melted. In large bowl dissolve yeast in the warm water. Add warm milk mixture and egg. Stir in enough flour to make a soft dough.
2. Turn dough out onto a lightly floured surface. Knead in enough remaining flour to make a moderately soft dough that is smooth and elastic (about 3 minutes total). Shape dough into a ball. Place in a lightly greased bowl; turn once to grease surface of dough. Cover; let rise in a warm place until double in size (about 1 hour).
3. Punch dough down. Turn dough out onto a lightly floured surface. Cover and let rest 10 minutes. Meanwhile, grease a 10-inch fluted tube pan.
4. Divide dough into 20 pieces. Flatten pieces into small circles. Top circles with cheese cubes, bacon, and green onion. Pull edges around cheese and pinch together to seal. Roll dough into balls. Place half the dough balls in prepared pan; brush with half the melted butter and sprinkle with 2 Tbsp. each cornmeal and Parmesan cheese. Add remaining dough balls. Brush with remaining butter and sprinkle with remaining cornmeal and Parmesan cheese. Cover; let rise in warm place until nearly double in size (about 30 minutes).
5. Preheat oven to 350°F. Bake 25 to 30 minutes or until bread sounds hollow when lightly tapped. Cool slightly. Remove from pan. If desired, drizzle with nacho cheese dip and serve warm. Makes 20 servings.
PER SERVING *200 cal., 8 g fat (5 g sat. fat), 31 mg chol., 254 mg sodium, 25 g carb., 1 g fiber, 6 g pro.*

ENGLISH MUFFINS IN A LOAF
WITH HONEY BUTTER

MAPLE-DATE-NUT
BREAD

MAPLE-DATE-NUT BREAD

PREP 20 minutes
BAKE 50 minutes at 350°F
COOL 15 minutes

1   cup all-purpose flour
1   cup whole wheat flour
1   tsp. baking powder
1   tsp. salt
¾   tsp. baking soda
1   cup boiling water
1   cup chopped pitted dates
1   Tbsp. butter, softened
¾   cup maple syrup
1   egg, lightly beaten
½   cup chopped pecans

1. Preheat oven to 350°F. Grease the bottom and ½ inch up the sides of an 8×4×2-inch loaf pan; set aside. In a large bowl combine flours, baking powder, salt, and baking soda. Make a well in center of flour mixture.
2. In a medium bowl pour the boiling water over dates and butter; stir until butter is melted. Cool 5 minutes. Stir maple syrup and egg into date mixture. Add egg mixture all at once to flour mixture. Stir just until moistened (batter should be lumpy). Fold pecans into batter. Pour into prepared pan.
3. Bake 50 to 60 minutes or until a wooden toothpick inserted near center comes out clean (if necessary cover loosely with foil the last 15 minutes of baking to prevent overbrowning).
4. Cool in pan on a wire rack 10 minutes. Remove from pan. Cool completely on rack. Wrap and store at least 8 hours before slicing. Makes 16 slices.
PER SLICE *159 cal., 4 g fat (1 g sat. fat), 15 mg chol., 231 mg sodium, 30 g carb., 2 g fiber, 3 g pro.*

RIBBONED BANANA BREAD

PREP 45 minutes
BAKE 70 minutes at 350°F
COOL 10 minutes

5   bananas (unpeeled)
½   8-oz. pkg. cream cheese, softened
1¼ cups sugar
1   egg yolk
2   cups plus 1 Tbsp. all-purpose flour
1   Tbsp. milk
1½ tsp. baking powder

1½ tsp. apple pie spice
½   tsp. baking soda
¼   tsp. salt
2   eggs, lightly beaten
½   cup vegetable oil

1. Preheat oven to 350°F. For roasted bananas, line a 15×10-inch baking pan with foil. Arrange bananas in pan. Prick unpeeled bananas with a fork at 1-inch intervals. Bake 15 minutes. Cool bananas in baking pan. Using a small sharp knife, split banana peels. Remove and lightly mash bananas. Measure 1½ cups roasted bananas.
2. Meanwhile, in a bowl beat cream cheese and ¼ cup of the sugar with a mixer on medium until combined. Beat in egg yolk, 1 Tbsp. flour, and the milk; set aside. Grease bottom and ½ inch up sides of a 9×5-inch loaf pan; set aside. In a large bowl combine remaining 2 cups flour, baking powder, apple pie spice, baking soda, and salt. Make a well in center of flour mixture; set aside.
3. In a medium bowl stir together remaining 1 cup sugar, eggs, and oil. Stir in roasted bananas. Add egg mixture all at once to flour mixture. Stir just until moistened (batter should be lumpy). Spoon half the batter into prepared pan. Top with cream cheese mixture; spread evenly. Drop remaining batter in spoonfuls over cream cheese layer; spread gently.
4. Bake 55 to 60 minutes or until a toothpick comes out clean (cover bread loosely with foil the last 15 minutes of baking if needed to prevent overbrowning) Cool in pan 10 minutes. Remove loaf from pan; cool on wire rack. Wrap and refrigerate at least 8 hours before slicing. Makes 16 slices.
PER SLICE *251 cal., 10 g fat (2 g sat. fat), 43 mg chol., 158 mg sodium, 37 g carb., 1 g fiber, 3 g pro.*

RIBBONED BANANA BREAD

SPICED BLUEBERRY MONKEY LOAVES

PREP 25 minutes
BAKE 35 minutes at 350°F
COOL 5 minutes
STAND 1 minute

- ¾ cup granulated sugar
- ¾ cup packed brown sugar
- 2 tsp. ground cinnamon
- 4 7.5-oz. pkg. refrigerated biscuits (40 biscuits total)
- 1½ cups fresh or frozen blueberries
- ½ cup butter, melted
- ⅓ cup rum or orange juice
- 1 tsp. vanilla

1. Preheat oven to 350°F. Lightly grease two 9×5-inch loaf pans. In an extra-large bowl stir together both sugars and cinnamon. Sprinkle 1 Tbsp. of the sugar mixture in each prepared pan.
2. Cut each biscuit into fourths. Add biscuit pieces, in batches, to sugar mixture, tossing to coat. Add blueberries; stir gently to mix. Divide biscuits and blueberries between the two loaf pans. Sprinkle with any remaining sugar mixture. Stir together butter, rum, and vanilla; pour over biscuits.
3. Bake 35 minutes or until the tops are golden brown and not doughy. Cool in pans 5 minutes. Run a knife around edge of pans; invert each pan onto a serving platter and let stand inverted 1 minute so topping covers loaves; remove pans. Cool slightly; serve warm. Makes 20 servings.
PER SERVING *242 cal., 10 g fat (4 g sat. fat), 12 mg chol., 464 mg sodium, 36 g carb., 1 g fiber, 2 g pro.*

CRANBERRY-PISTACHIO ROLLS

PREP 30 minutes
BAKE 15 minutes at 350°F
STAND 2 minutes

- ½ cup sugar
- ⅓ cup finely chopped dried cranberries
- ⅓ cup finely chopped or ground pistachios
- 1 tsp. lemon or orange zest
- 2 8-ounce pkg. refrigerated dough sheets (such as Pillsbury Recipe Creations seamless dough sheet)
- ¼ cup butter, softened
- 1 recipe Zesty Lemon Powdered Sugar Glaze

1. Preheat oven to 350°F. Grease twelve 2½-inch muffin cups.
2. Combine sugar, cranberries, pistachios, and lemon zest. Unroll dough sheets; spread each with half of the softened butter. Working with a long side toward you, sprinkle cranberry-pistachio mixture over dough; press down gently. Fold bottom third of dough up over filling. Fold over again. Pinch along seam to seal.
3. Cut each rectangle crosswise into 12 strips. Fold each strip in half; arrange, cut sides up, in each prepared cup. Sprinkle any cranberry-pistachio mixture that falls from rolls over rolls in muffin cups.
4. Bake 15 minutes or until tops are lightly golden. Let stand 2 minutes. Remove from cups. Drizzle with Zesty Lemon Powdered Sugar Glaze. Makes 12 servings.
Zesty Lemon Powdered Sugar Glaze Stir together 1 cup powdered sugar, 4 tsp. milk, and 1 tsp. lemon or orange zest until combined.
PER SERVING *256 cal., 10 g fat (5 g sat. fat), 10 mg chol., 345 mg sodium, 38 g carb., 1 g fiber, 3 g pro.*

CRANBERRY-PISTACHIO ROLLS

SPICED
BLUEBERRY
MONKEY
LOAVES

3. Bake 30 minutes. Sprinkle bread with remaining ¼ cup cheese. Cover with foil and bake 5 minutes more or until a toothpick comes out clean, top is golden brown, and cheese is melted. Cool in pan 10 minutes. Remove bread from pan. If desired, sprinkle with fresh basil. Serve warm. Makes 16 servings.

PER SERVING *273 cal., 16 g fat (6 g sat. fat), 20 mg chol., 784 mg sodium, 26 g carb., 1 g fiber, 7 g pro.*

CHEESE POPOVERS

PREP 30 minutes
BAKE 35 minutes at 400°F

　　Shortening
2¾　cups milk
10　eggs, at room temperature
3　cups all-purpose flour
1½　Tbsp. sugar
3　tsp. kosher salt
3　oz. dry Monterey Jack cheese, shredded (¾ cup)

1. Position oven rack in center of oven. Preheat oven to 400°F. Grease 12 popover pans.
2. In a medium saucepan bring milk to steaming (160°F). In large bowl lightly beat eggs. Slowly add 1 cup of the hot milk to eggs, stirring until combined. Pour egg mixture into saucepan. Stir to combine. Strain mixture through a fine-mesh sieve into a large bowl. Sift the flour, sugar, and salt over the egg mixture. With a mixer, beat on lowest speed 10 minutes. Increase speed to medium-low and beat 5 minutes more. Strain mixture through a fine-mesh sieve.
3. Place empty popover pan in oven until pan is hot (about 5 minutes). Working quickly, fill pans three-fourths full. Sprinkle with cheese. Immediately return pan to oven and bake 35 minutes or until popovers are deep golden brown (to prevent them from collapsing do not open oven door while popovers bake). Remove from baking pan; place on wire rack to cool. Immediately pierce sides of popovers with a skewer to allow steam to escape. Makes 12 servings.

PER SERVING *245 cal., 9 g fat (3 g sat. fat), 183 mg chol., 612 mg sodium, 29 g carb., 1 g fiber, 12 g pro.*

EASY SAUSAGE-PESTO RING

EASY SAUSAGE-PESTO RING

PREP 20 minutes
BAKE 35 minutes at 350°F
COOL 10 minutes

5　Tbsp. butter, melted
2　16.3-oz. pkg. refrigerated biscuits (16 biscuits)
⅓　cup basil pesto
⅓　cup cooked and crumbled bulk Italian sausage (about 3 oz.)

1¼　cups shredded Italian cheese blend
　　Fresh snipped basil or Italian parsley (optional)

1. Preheat oven to 350°F. Grease a 10-inch fluted tube pan with 3 Tbsp. of the butter.
2. Top each biscuit with 1 tsp. pesto, 1 tsp. sausage, and 1 Tbsp. cheese. Stack four biscuits; press down gently. Turn stack on its side and place in pan. Repeat with remaining biscuits, arranging biscuit stacks in pan to create a ring. Drizzle with remaining 2 Tbsp. melted butter.

APPLE-CARROT CAKE MUFFINS

PREP 25 minutes
BAKE 20 minutes at 350°F
COOL 10 minutes

2   cups all-purpose flour
1¼   cups sugar
2   tsp. baking soda
1   to 1½ tsp. apple pie spice
½   tsp. salt
2   cups finely shredded carrots
1   cup shredded, peeled apple
½   cup raisins
3   eggs, lightly beaten
⅔   cup vegetable oil
⅓   cup milk
1   tsp. vanilla
1   recipe Coconut Streusel (optional)

1. Preheat oven to 350°F. Grease twenty-four 2½-inch muffin cups or line with paper bake cups.
2. In a large bowl combine the first five ingredients (through salt). Make a well in center of flour mixture; set aside. In another bowl combine carrots, apple, and raisins.
3. In a medium bowl combine eggs, oil, milk, and vanilla. Stir in carrot mixture. Add egg mixture all at once to flour mixture. Stir just until moistened (batter should be lumpy). Spoon batter into prepared cups, filling each about three-fourths full. If desired, sprinkle with Coconut Streusel.
4. Bake 20 to 25 minutes or until golden. Cool 10 minutes in muffin cups. Remove from cups. Serve warm or cool. Makes 24 servings.
PER SERVING *161 cal., 7 g fat (1 g sat. fat), 24 mg chol., 172 mg sodium, 23 g carb., 1 g fiber, 2 g pro*

Coconut Streusel In a bowl combine ¼ cup all-purpose flour and ¼ cup packed brown sugar. Using a pastry blender, cut in ¼ cup cold butter, cut up. Stir in ½ cup shredded coconut.

APPLE-CARROT CAKE MUFFINS

MAPLE-BACON
CORN MUFFINS

MAPLE-BACON CORN MUFFINS

PREP 15 minutes
BAKE 20 minutes at 350°F
COOL 5 minutes

      Nonstick cooking spray
1   cup yellow cornmeal
¾   cup all-purpose flour
1   Tbsp. baking powder
¾   tsp. salt
2   eggs, lightly beaten
¾   cup maple syrup
¾   cup milk
¼   cup plain low-fat yogurt
3   Tbsp. vegetable oil
10   slices crisp-cooked bacon,
      crumbled

1. Preheat oven to 350°F. Line fifteen 2½-inch muffin cups with paper bake cups; coat paper cups with cooking spray. Set aside.
2. In a medium bowl stir together cornmeal, flour, baking powder, and salt. Make a well in center of cornmeal mixture. In a bowl combine eggs, maple syrup, milk, yogurt, and oil. Add egg mixture all at once to cornmeal mixture. Stir just until moistened. Fold in eight crumbled bacon slices.
3. Spoon batter into the prepared muffin cups, filling each two-thirds full. Bake 20 to 25 minutes or until a toothpick inserted in centers comes out clean. Cool on wire racks 5 minutes. Remove from muffin cups. Top with remaining two crumbled bacon slices. Serve warm. If desired, serve with additional maple syrup. Makes 15 servings.

PER SERVING *172 cal., 6 g fat (1 g sat. fat), 32 mg chol., 326 mg sodium, 24 g carb., 1 g fiber, 5 g pro.*

TOASTED COCONUT AND CHOCOLATE CHIP SCONES

PREP 20 minutes
BAKE 18 minutes at 400°F

1   cup shredded unsweetened
      coconut
2¼   cups all-purpose flour
1   Tbsp. sugar
1   Tbsp. baking powder
¼   tsp. salt
6   Tbsp. cold butter
1   egg, lightly beaten

TOASTED COCONUT AND CHOCOLATE CHIP SCONES

¾   cup heavy cream
1   cup semi-sweet chocolate pieces

1. Preheat oven to 400°F. Spread 1 cup coconut on a baking sheet. Bake 5 to 7 minutes or until golden, stirring once. Cool slightly. Transfer to a food processor. Process until finely ground; set aside.
2. In a large bowl combine flour, sugar, baking powder, and salt. Using a pastry blender, cut in butter until mixture resembles coarse crumbs. Make a well in center of flour mixture; set aside.
3. In a medium bowl combine egg and heavy cream. Add egg mixture all at once to flour mixture. Add finely ground toasted coconut and chocolate pieces. Using a fork, stir just until moistened.

4. Turn dough out onto a lightly floured surface. Knead dough by folding and gently pressing 10 to 12 strokes or until dough is nearly smooth. Pat dough into a 10×4-inch rectangle. Cut in half lengthwise and in sixths crosswise to make 12 rectangles.
5. Place rectangles 2 inches apart on an ungreased baking sheet. Brush with additional cream. Bake 13 to 15 minutes or until golden brown. If desired, top with additional shredded coconut the last 5 minutes of baking. Remove scones from baking sheet. Serve warm. Makes 12 servings.

PER SERVING *305 cal., 19 g fat (12 g sat. fat), 55 mg chol., 248 mg sodium, 32 g carb., 2 g fiber, 4 g pro.*

PARMESAN-PECAN SHORTBREAD

PREP 25 minutes
CHILL 8 hours
BAKE 15 minutes at 325°F

¾ cup butter, softened
2 cups finely shredded Parmesan cheese (8 oz.)
1¼ cups all-purpose flour
1 Tbsp. paprika
¼ tsp. cayenne pepper
1 cup finely chopped pecans
2 Tbsp. snipped fresh chives
  Apricot preserves (optional)

1. In a large bowl beat butter with a mixer on medium 1 minute. Stir in cheese. Stir in flour, paprika, and cayenne pepper until combined. Stir in pecans and chives to form a crumbly dough.
2. Turn dough out onto a lightly floured surface. Gently knead dough 1 minute. Shape into a 12-inch log. Wrap log in plastic wrap; chill 8 hours.
3. Preheat oven to 325°F. Using a serrated knife, cut log into ¼-inch slices. Place slices 1 inch apart on an ungreased parchment-lined cookie sheet. Bake 15 to 17 minutes or until set. Remove rounds; cool on a wire rack. If desired, serve with apricot preserves. Makes 36 servings.
PER SERVING *103 cal., 7 g fat (3 g sat. fat), 13 mg chol., 103 mg sodium, 8 g carb., 1 g fiber, 3 g pro.*

EVERYTHING CRACKER CRISPS

PREP 30 minutes
REST 30 minutes
BAKE 8 minutes at 450°F

¼ cup sesame seeds
¼ cup poppy seeds
2 Tbsp. dried minced garlic, crushed
2 Tbsp. dried minced onion, crushed
1¼ cups all-purpose flour
1 cup whole wheat flour
1½ tsp. baking powder
1½ tsp. salt
3 Tbsp. vegetable oil
¾ cup plus 3 Tbsp. water

1. In a small dry skillet stir sesame and poppy seeds over medium heat for 1 to 2 minutes or until toasted. Remove from heat. Stir in garlic and onion; cool.
2. In a large bowl combine garlic, onion, both flours, baking powder, and salt; stir in seed mixture and oil. Add the water; stir just until moistened. Turn dough out onto a lightly floured surface and knead five times or until smooth. Divide dough into eight portions. Cover and let rest 30 minutes.
3. Preheat oven to 450°F. Line a baking sheet with parchment paper. Roll one portion of dough at a time into an 11×5-inch rectangle; transfer to prepared baking sheet. Bake 8 minutes or until brown and crisp, turning once halfway through. Remove; cool on a wire rack. Break into pieces. Store at room temperature up to 5 days. Makes 36 servings.
PER SERVING *50 cal., 2 g fat (0 g sat. fat), 0 mg chol., 118 mg sodium, 7 g carb., 1 g fiber, 1 g pro.*

PARMESAN-PECAN
SHORTBREAD

EVERYTHING
CRACKER CRISPS

Something Sweet

If there is a perfect time to indulge in something sweet and spectacular, it is during the Christmas season. These cakes, pies, puddings, parfaits, and pastries will make you look forward to the holidays all year long.

SNICKERDOODLE
CHEESECAKE,
PAGE 84

COCONUT-CARROT
CAKE

COCONUT-CARROT CAKE

PREP 30 minutes
BAKE 25 minutes at 350°F
COOL 15 minutes

- 1¾ cups granulated sugar, plus more for pans
- 2½ cups all-purpose flour
- 2 tsp. ground cinnamon
- 2 tsp. baking powder
- 1 tsp. baking soda
- ¾ tsp. salt
- 4 eggs, lightly beaten
- 2 Tbsp. grated fresh ginger
- 1 cup vegetable oil or canola oil
- 3 cups grated carrots
- ½ cup chopped pecans
- 1½ cups flaked coconut, toasted (tip, page 20)
- 1 8-oz. cream cheese, softened
- ¾ cup butter, softened
- 1 lb. powdered sugar (4 cups)
- 1 tsp. vanilla extract
  Large coconut shavings, toasted (tip, page 20)

1. Preheat oven to 350°F. Grease three 8-inch round cake pans; line bottoms with parchment paper. Grease and sprinkle with granulated sugar; tap out excess. In a bowl stir together flour, cinnamon, baking powder, baking soda, and salt.
2. In a bowl combine eggs and 1¾ cups granulated sugar. Stir in ginger and oil. Stir in flour mixture until combined. Fold in carrots, pecans, and toasted coconut. Divide batter among prepared pans.
3. Bake 25 to 30 minutes or until cakes spring back when lightly touched in center. Cool layers in pans on wire racks 15 minutes. Remove cakes from pans; peel off parchment paper. Cool completely on wire racks.
4. Meanwhile, for frosting, in a large bowl beat cream cheese and butter with a mixer on medium until smooth. Add powdered sugar and vanilla; beat just until combined and smooth.
5. Place one cake layer, bottom side up, on a serving plate. Spread with 1 cup of frosting. Top with second cake layer, bottom side up. Spread with another 1 cup of frosting. Top with remaining layer, top side up; spread top of cake with remaining frosting. Sprinkle with toasted coconut shavings. Makes 16 servings.
PER SERVING 602 cal., 33 g fat (12 g sat. fat), 85 mg chol., 426 mg sodium, 74 g carb., 2 g fiber, 5 g pro.

YELLOW CAKE WITH SALTED CHOCOLATE GANACHE

YELLOW CAKE WITH SALTED CHOCOLATE GANACHE

PREP 50 minutes
BAKE 35 minutes at 350°F
COOL 10 minutes

- 3 cups all-purpose flour
- 2½ tsp. baking powder
- 1 tsp. kosher salt
- 2 cups sugar
- 1 cup butter, at room temperature
- 4 eggs plus 2 egg yolks, at room temperature
- 1 tsp. vanilla
- 1 cup buttermilk, room temperature
- 1 recipe Salted Dark Chocolate Ganache
  Sea salt

1. Preheat oven to 350°F. Grease and flour two 9×2-inch round baking pans; set aside. In a medium bowl sift together flour, baking powder, and salt. In an extra-large bowl beat sugar and butter with a mixer on medium to high 6 to 8 minutes or until very light and fluffy. Add eggs and yolks, one at a time, beating until combined after each addition. Beat in vanilla. Add flour mixture to butter mixture in three additions, alternating with buttermilk. Divide batter between prepared pans, filling each about half full (3¼ cups batter). Spread batter in pans.
2. Bake 35 minutes or until a toothpick inserted near center comes out clean. Remove; cool in pans on wire rack 10 minutes. Remove from pans and cool completely. Frost with Salted Dark Chocolate Ganache. Sprinkle with sea salt. Makes 16 servings.
Salted Dark Chocolate Ganache Place 16-oz. chopped dark chocolate in a large heatproof bowl. In a medium saucepan bring 1 cup heavy cream just to boiling. Pour cream over chocolate. Let stand without stirring 2 minutes. Stir to melt chocolate. Stir in ¼ tsp. kosher salt. Set bowl in a larger bowl with ice water 15 to 20 minutes or until cool, stirring occasionally. Beat with a mixer on medium 2 minutes or until light and fluffy. Spread over cake layers.
PER SERVING 565 cal., 36 g fat (22 g sat. fat), 143 mg chol., 369 mg sodium, 61 g carb., 3 g fiber, 7 g pro.

CHOCOLATE-
HAZELNUT BACON
LAYER CAKE

CHOCOLATE-
HAZELNUT BACON
LAYER CAKE

PREP 45 minutes
BAKE 30 minutes at 350°F
COOL 1 hour

Unsweetened cocoa powder
1   cup all-purpose flour
1   cup sugar
¾   cup unsweetened cocoa powder
1   tsp. baking soda
½   tsp. baking powder
½   tsp. salt
2   eggs
¾   cup water
¾   cup buttermilk or sour milk*
⅓   cup vegetable oil
8   slices bacon, crisp-cooked and
     crumbled

½   cup chocolate-hazelnut spread,
     warmed
⅓   cup chopped toasted hazelnuts
1   recipe Ganache

1. Preheat oven to 350°F. Grease two
8-inch round cake pans and dust with
cocoa powder; set aside. In a large bowl
stir together the next six ingredients
(through salt). Whisk together eggs,
the water, buttermilk, and oil. Add egg
mixture to flour mixture all at once; whisk
until smooth. Stir in half of bacon. Pour
batter into pans (batter will be thin).
2. Bake 30 minutes or until a toothpick
comes out clean. Cool in pans 10 minutes.
Remove cakes from pans; cool
completely on wire racks.
3. For filling, in a bowl combine chocolate-
hazelnut spread, the remaining bacon,
and hazelnuts.

4. Place one cake layer on a platter.
Spread with filling. Add remaining cake
layer. Spread top with Ganache, allowing
it to drip down sides of cake. If desired, top
with additional crumbled cooked bacon
and chopped toasted hazelnuts. Makes
16 servings.
Ganache In a small saucepan heat ½ cup
heavy cream just until simmering. Pour over
6 oz. semisweet chocolate pieces (do not
stir). Let stand 5 minutes. Stir until smooth.
Cool 15 minutes or to desired consistency.
*Tip For ¾ cup sour milk, place 2 tsp. lemon
juice or vinegar in a glass measuring cup.
Add milk to equal ¾ cup; stir. Let stand
5 minutes.
PER SERVING *301 cal., 18 g fat (6 g sat. fat),
39 mg chol., 262 mg sodium, 34 g carb.,
3 g fiber, 6 g pro.*

CARAMEL-FROSTED HUMMINGBIRD CAKE

PREP 30 minutes
BAKE 40 minutes at 350°F
COOL 2 hours

3 cups all-purpose flour
2 cups sugar
2 tsp. baking powder
1 tsp. salt
½ tsp. baking soda
½ tsp. ground cinnamon
2 cups mashed ripe bananas
1 8-oz. can crushed pineapple (juice pack)
1 cup vegetable oil
3 eggs, lightly beaten
½ cup flaked coconut
1½ tsp. vanilla
1 recipe Salty Caramel Cream Cheese Frosting

1. Preheat oven to 350°F. Lightly grease and flour a 13×9-inch baking pan.
2. In an extra-large bowl stir together the first six ingredients (through cinnamon). Add bananas, undrained pineapple, oil, eggs, coconut, and vanilla, stirring just until combined. Spread batter into prepared pan.
3. Bake 40 to 45 minutes or until a toothpick comes out clean. Cool cake completely in pan on a wire rack. Frost cake with Salty Caramel Cream Cheese Frosting. Makes 16 servings.
Salty Caramel Cream Cheese Frosting In a large bowl beat 4 oz. softened cream cheese, ¼ cup softened butter, ¼ cup caramel-flavor ice cream topping, 1 tsp. vanilla, and ¼ tsp. salt with a mixer on medium until light and fluffy. Gradually beat in 2¾ to 3 cups powdered sugar to reach spreading consistency.
PER SERVING 513 cal., 21 g fat (6 g sat. fat), 50 mg chol., 371 mg sodium, 79 g carb., 1 g fiber, 5 g pro.

STOUT GINGERBREAD WITH CITRUS HARD SAUCE

PREP 25 minutes
STAND 15 minutes
BAKE 40 minutes at 350°F
COOL 10 minutes

Nonstick spray for baking
¾ cup stout beer (such as Guinness)
2½ cups all-purpose flour
1 Tbsp. ground ginger
2 tsp. ground cinnamon
1½ tsp. baking powder
½ tsp. baking soda
½ tsp. salt
¼ tsp. freshly grated nutmeg or ⅛ tsp. ground nutmeg
¼ tsp. ground cardamom
1 cup butter, softened
1¼ cups packed brown sugar
3 eggs
1 cup mild-flavor molasses
1 Tbsp. grated fresh ginger
1 Tbsp. powdered sugar
1 recipe Citrus Hard Sauce*

1. Preheat oven to 350°F. Generously coat a 10-inch fluted tube pan with nonstick spray for baking. Pour beer into a measuring cup; let stand at room temperature 15 minutes. In a bowl combine flour, ginger, cinnamon, baking powder, and baking soda, salt, nutmeg, and cardamom.
2. In a large bowl beat butter with a mixer on medium 30 seconds. Gradually add brown sugar, ¼ cup at a time, beating on medium until combined. Scrape bowl; beat 2 minutes more. Add eggs, one at a time, beating well after each addition. Stir in molasses and grated ginger. Alternately add flour mixture and beer, beating after each addition until combined.
3. Pour batter into prepared pan. Bake 40 to 50 minutes or until a toothpick comes out clean. Cool cake in pan on wire rack 10 minutes; remove from pan. Sprinkle with powdered sugar. Serve warm with Citrus Hard Sauce. Makes 12 servings.
Citrus Hard Sauce In a bowl beat ¼ cup softened butter with a mixer on medium until light and fluffy. Beat in ¾ cup powdered sugar, 2 Tbsp. orange liqueur, 2 tsp. orange zest, and 1 tsp. vanilla until smooth.
* Citrus Hard Sauce is best when chilled 24 hours before serving.
PER SERVING 496 cal., 21 g fat (13 g sat. fat), 104 mg chol., 366 mg sodium, 73 g carb., 1 g fiber, 5 g pro.

STOUT GINGERBREAD WITH CITRUS HARD SAUCE

SNOW GLOBE CUPCAKES

PREP 1 hour
BAKE 20 minutes at 350°F
COOL 45 minutes

- 3 cups Creamy White Frosting
  Blue food coloring
- 12 2½-inch cupcakes in paper bake cups
  Clear and/or blue coarse sugar (optional)
  Tiny marshmallows; assorted colors rolled fruit leather; black candy-coated chocolate pieces

(such as M&Ms and Sixlets); multicolor confetti sprinkles and nonpareils; orange gumdrops cut into slivers; snowflake sprinkles
- 12 creme-filled chocolate sandwich cookies

1. Tint half the Creamy White Frosting a light sky blue color with blue food coloring. Spread top half of each cupcake with blue frosting for sky, swirling slightly. Spread bottom half with white frosting for snow, swirling slightly. If desired, roll edges of cupcakes in coarse sugar.

2. For each snowman cupcake, press two tiny marshmallows together and flatten to a disk. Flatten a single tiny marshmallow to a smaller disk. Position small disk above the large disk on a frosted cupcake to create a snowman.

3. For snowman scarves, unroll red and blue fruit leather and cut into strips. Decorate each snowman with a scarf. Press candy-coated chocolate pieces into frosting for a hat. For another style of hat, cut a triangle from yellow fruit leather. Attach nonpareils for eyes and a gumdrop sliver for a nose. Cut triangles from green fruit leather. Decorate with

snowflake sprinkles around snowman for a winter scene.

4. To make cupcakes look like snow globes, place each cupcake on its side on a creme-filled chocolate sandwich cookie. Secure cupcakes to cookies with white frosting. Makes 12 servings.

Creamy White Frosting In a large bowl beat 1 cup shortening, 1½ tsp. clear vanilla extract, and ½ tsp. almond extract with a mixer on medium 30 seconds. Gradually add 2 cups powdered sugar, beating well. Add 2 Tbsp. milk. Gradually beat in 2 cups powdered sugar. Gradually add milk, 1 Tbsp. at a time, until frosting reaches spreading consistency (3 to 4 Tbsp. total). Makes about 3 cups.

Snow Globe Cupcakes with Christmas Trees Frost cupcakes as directed in Step 1. For trees, unroll green rolled fruit leather and cut into triangles. Press trees onto frosted cupcakes. Attach multicolor confetti sprinkles or nonpareils on trees with frosting. If desired, make cupcakes look like snow globes as directed in Step 4.

Snow Globe Cupcakes with Gingerbread People Frost cupcakes as directed in Step 1. For each gingerbread person, in a microwave-safe bowl heat two or three vanilla caramels, unwrapped, on high for 5 to 10 seconds or until softened. Press caramels together into a flat disk; cut out a gingerbread person with a 1-inch cutter. Pipe white frosting zig-zags onto arms and legs; pipe hair, eyes, and nose. With frosting, attach small red decorative candies for buttons. Press onto cupcake. If desired, make cupcakes look like snow globes as directed in Step 4.

PER SERVING *563 cal., 26 g fat (11 g sat. fat), 72 mg chol., 352 mg sodium, 80 g carb., 1 g fiber, 5 g pro.*

UPSIDE-DOWN RED VELVET PUDDING CAKES

PREP 30 minutes
COOL 15 minutes
FREEZE 1 hour
BAKE 20 minutes at 375°F
STAND 10 minutes

1   cup milk chocolate pieces
⅓   cup heavy cream
1   Tbsp. butter
¼   cup butter

UPSIDE-DOWN RED VELVET PUDDING CAKES

1   egg
    Nonstick cooking spray
1   cup all-purpose flour
1   tsp. unsweetened cocoa powder
¼   tsp. salt
¾   cup sugar
2   tsp. red food coloring
½   tsp. vanilla
½   cup buttermilk or sour milk*
½   tsp. baking soda
½   tsp. vinegar
    Chocolate curls (optional)

1. For filling, in a small saucepan, combine chocolate pieces, cream, and 1 Tbsp. butter. Stir over low heat until chocolate is melted. Transfer to a small bowl. Cool 15 minutes, stirring occasionally. Cover and freeze 1 hour or until fudgelike consistency.

2. Meanwhile, allow ¼ cup butter and egg to stand at room temperature 30 minutes. Preheat oven to 375°F. Coat eight 6-oz. custard cups or ramekins with cooking spray; arrange in a 15×10×1-inch baking pan. In a bowl stir together flour, cocoa powder, and salt.

3. In a medium bowl beat ¼ cup butter with a mixer on medium to high 30 seconds. Gradually add sugar, beating on medium until combined. Beat 2 minutes more, scraping side of bowl occasionally. Beat in egg, food coloring, and vanilla. Alternately add flour mixture and buttermilk, beating on low after each addition or just until combined. In a bowl combine baking soda and vinegar; stir into batter.

4. Divide half the batter among prepared custard cups. Divide filling into eight portions. Working quickly, use hands to roll each portion into a ball. Place a ball of filling on batter in each cup; do not allow filling to touch sides of cups. Spoon remaining batter into custard cups.

5. Bake 20 minutes or until tops spring back when lightly touched. Remove from oven. Let stand 10 minutes. Using a knife, loosen cakes from sides of cups; invert onto dessert plates. Spoon any filling in cups on cakes. If desired, top with chocolate curls. Makes 8 servings.

* For ½ cup sour milk, place 1½ tsp. lemon juice or vinegar in a glass measuring cup. Add milk to equal ½ cup total liquid; stir. Let stand 5 minutes.

PER SERVING *386 cal., 21 g fat (13 g sat. fat), 65 mg chol., 256 mg sodium, 50 g carb., 2 g fiber, 5 g pro.*

TIRAMISU PARFAITS

PREP 25 minutes
BAKE 12 minutes at 350°F
CHILL 30 minutes

- 2 6-oz. cartons low-fat plain Greek yogurt
- 1 8-oz. carton mascarpone cheese, softened
- 2 Tbsp. honey
- 1 tsp. instant espresso powder
- 1 10.75-oz. loaf pound cake, cut into 1-inch cubes
- ¼ cup dry marsala or dry sherry
- 1 oz. dark chocolate, grated (⅓ cup)
  - 2 cups fresh raspberries

1. In a bowl combine yogurt, mascarpone, honey, and espresso powder. Cover and chill at least 30 minutes.
2. Meanwhile, preheat oven to 350°F. Place pound cake cubes in an even layer in a 15×10×1-inch baking pan. Bake 12 minutes or until lightly toasted, stirring once. Cool in baking pan on a wire rack.

3. Divide half the pound cake cubes among eight to ten 8- to 9-oz. glasses. Drizzle with half the marsala. Top with half the yogurt mixture, grated chocolate, and raspberries. Repeat layers. If desired, drizzle parfaits with additional honey. Serve within 1 hour. Makes 8 servings.
PER SERVING 397 cal., 22 g fat (12 g sat. fat), 98 mg chol., 135 mg sodium, 39 g carb., 3 g fiber, 8 g pro.

DOUBLE-CHOCOLATE-ESPRESSO TRUFFLE PIE

PREP 40 minutes
BAKE 14 minutes at 450°F
CHILL 8 hours

- 1½ cups all-purpose flour
- 3 Tbsp. unsweetened cocoa powder
- 2 Tbsp. packed brown sugar
- ½ tsp. salt
- ½ cup butter, cut up
- 5 Tbsp. cold water
- 2 cups heavy cream
- 6 oz. 60% to 70% dark chocolate or bittersweet chocolate, chopped
- 1 cup granulated sugar
- 6 egg yolks, lightly beaten
- 3 Tbsp. brewed espresso or strong brewed coffee
- 1 tsp. vanilla
  Sweetened whipped cream
  Chopped espresso beans (optional)

1. Preheat oven to 450°F. For chocolate pastry, in a food processor, combine flour, cocoa powder, brown sugar, and salt. Cover; process just until combined. Add butter. Cover; pulse until butter pieces are peasize. With processor running, quickly add the water through feed tube just until dough comes together. Transfer dough to a large bowl; gather into a ball, kneading gently until it holds together. Gently pat dough into a disk.
2. On a lightly floured surface, roll dough from center to edges into a 12-inch circle. Wrap pastry circle around rolling pin; unroll into a 9-inch glass pie plate. Ease pastry into pie plate without stretching. Trim pastry to ½ inch beyond edge of pie plate. Fold under extra pastry even with edge of plate. Crimp edge as desired. Using a fork, prick bottom and side of pastry shell, and where bottom and side meet. Line pastry with a double thickness of foil.
3. Bake 8 minutes; remove foil. Bake 6 to 8 minutes more or until pastry is set and looks dry. Cool on a wire rack.
4. For chocolate filling, in a medium-size heavy saucepan, combine heavy cream, chocolate, and granulated sugar. Cook and stir over medium heat 10 minutes or until mixture comes to boiling and thickens. (If chocolate flecks remain, use a wire whisk to beat mixture until blended.)
5. Gradually stir about half the hot mixture into egg yolks. Return egg yolk mixture to saucepan. Cook and stir 2 minutes. Remove from heat; stir in espresso and vanilla. Cool slightly. Pour warm filling into baked pie pastry shell. Cover and chill 8 to 24 hours or until filling is set.
6. Top pie with whipped cream, and, if desired, top with chopped espresso beans. Makes 10 servings.
PER SERVING 579 cal., 41 g fat (24 g sat. fat), 217 mg chol., 229 mg sodium, 49 g carb., 2 g fiber, 6 g pro.

TIRAMISU PARFAITS

DOUBLE-CHOCOLATE-
ESPRESSO TRUFFLE PIE

BUTTERMILK-
CARDAMOM
PUMPKIN PIE

BUTTERMILK-CARDAMOM PUMPKIN PIE

PREP 40 minutes
BAKE 45 minutes at 350°F

1   recipe Baked Piecrust
2   Tbsp. sugar
1¼   tsp. ground cardamom
1   cup sugar
3   Tbsp. all-purpose flour
¼   tsp. salt
1   15-oz. can pumpkin
3   eggs, lightly beaten
½   cup buttermilk
¼   cup butter, melted
1   tsp. vanilla bean paste

1. Preheat oven to 350°F. Prepare Baked Piecrust; set aside. In a small bowl combine 2 Tbsp. sugar and 1 tsp. cardamom; set aside. In a large bowl combine the 1 cup sugar, flour, salt, and the remaining ¼ tsp. cardamom; mix well. Add pumpkin and mix well. Add eggs; stir to combine.
2. Combine buttermilk, melted butter, and vanilla bean paste. Gradually add to pumpkin mixture, stirring just until combined. Carefully pour filling into baked pastry shell; sprinkle with half the sugar-cardamom. Cover edges to prevent overbrowning. Bake 45 to 50 minutes or until center appears set when gently shaken. Cool on a wire rack. Chill within 2 hours. Sprinkle with remaining sugar-cardamom. Makes 8 servings.

Baked Piecrust In a medium bowl combine 1¼ cups all-purpose flour, 1 tsp. sugar, and ½ tsp. salt. Use a pastry blender to cut in ⅓ cup butter (cut into cubes), and 2 Tbsp. shortening until pea-size. Add 1 Tbsp. water over a portion of the flour mixture, tossing gently with a fork. Move moistened dough to side of bowl and continue with remaining water until all dough is moistened (4 to 5 Tbsp. water total). Knead together dough in about six to eight strokes until it holds together. Wrap dough in plastic wrap and chill 30 minutes. Preheat oven to 425°F. Roll dough on a lightly floured surface into a 13-inch circle. Fold dough into quarters and transfer to a 9-inch pie plate; unfold. Trim edges of pastry about ½ inch beyond edge of pie plate. Fold

TANGY GRAPEFRUIT TART

extra pastry under itself to form the edge. Crimp edge of piecrust as desired. Poke sides and bottom of crust with a fork. Line pastry with a double thickness of foil and weight dough with pie weights or dried beans. Bake crust 10 to 12 minutes or until dry and set. Carefully remove foil and weights and bake another 3 to 4 minutes or until very lightly brown. Cool completely.
PER SERVING *395 cal., 19 g fat (10 g sat. fat), 106 mg chol., 371 mg sodium, 52 g carb., 2 g fiber, 6 g pro.*

TANGY GRAPEFRUIT TART

PREP 30 minutes
BAKE 5 minutes at 400°F
COOL 30 minutes
CHILL 4 hours

1   purchased graham cracker crumb pie shell
1   egg white, lightly beaten
¾   cup sugar
3   Tbsp. cornstarch
1½   cups grapefruit juice
3   egg yolks
6   Tbsp. butter, cut up
1   drop red food coloring
¼   cup coconut, toasted (tip, page 20)
2   Tbsp. chopped dry-roasted pistachio nuts

1. Preheat oven to 400°F. Lightly brush crust with egg white. Bake 5 minutes or until lightly browned. Cool at least 30 minutes.
2. For filling, in a medium saucepan stir together sugar and cornstarch. Add juice; cook and stir over medium heat until thickened and bubbly. Gradually whisk half the mixture into egg yolks. Return mixture to saucepan. Cook and stir constantly until filling boils gently. Cook and stir 2 minutes more. Remove from heat. Add butter and stir until melted. Stir in food coloring. Pour filling into crust.
3. Cover tart loosely and chill 4 to 6 hours or until set. Top with coconut and pistachios. Makes 10 servings.
PER SERVING *262 cal., 14 g fat (7 g sat. fat), 74 mg chol., 170 mg sodium, 34 g carb., 1 g fiber, 3 g pro.*

SNICKERDOODLE CHEESECAKE (PHOTO, PAGE 73)

STAND 30 minutes
PREP 25 minutes
BAKE 40 minutes at 350°F
COOL 2 hours
CHILL 4 hours

2   8-oz. pkg. cream cheese
3   eggs, lightly beaten
1   10-oz. pkg. shortbread cookies, finely crushed
1   Tbsp. sugar
¼   cup butter, melted
1   8-oz. carton sour cream
1   cup sugar
2   Tbsp. all-purpose flour
2   tsp. vanilla
1   tsp. ground cinnamon
1   Tbsp. sugar

1. Allow cream cheese and eggs to stand at room temperature 30 minutes. Preheat oven to 350°F. For crust, in a bowl stir together crushed cookies and 1 Tbsp. sugar. Stir in melted butter until combined. Press crust onto the bottom and 1½ inches up sides of a 9-inch springform pan.
2. In a large bowl beat cream cheese, sour cream, 1 cup sugar, flour, vanilla, and ½ tsp. cinnamon with a mixer on medium until smooth. Stir in eggs.

3. In a bowl stir together 1 Tbsp. sugar and the remaining ½ tsp. cinnamon. Pour filling into crust-lined pan; spread evenly. Sprinkle with cinnamon-sugar mixture. Place springform pan in a shallow baking pan.
4. Bake 40 to 50 minutes or until a 2½-inch area around edge appears set when gently shaken. Cool in springform pan on a wire rack 15 minutes. Using a small sharp knife, loosen crust from sides of pan. Cool 30 minutes more. Remove sides of pan; cool cheesecake completely on wire rack. Cover and chill at least 4 hours. If desired, make a star-shape cardboard stencil and decorate with additional cinnamon-sugar. Makes 12 servings.
PER SERVING *412 cal., 27 g fat (14 g sat. fat), 108 mg chol., 310 mg sodium, 39 g carb., 5 g pro.*

BACON-CHEDDAR COUNTRY APPLE TART

PREP 25 minutes
CHILL 1 hour
BAKE 40 minutes at 375°F
COOL 1 hour

4   slices bacon
1½ cups all-purpose flour
¼   tsp. salt
⅓   cup shortening
5   to 6 Tbsp. cold water
¼   cup apple jelly
4   cups sliced, peeled cooking apples, (such as Rome, Jonagold, Braeburn, and/or Honeycrisp)
       Milk
       Sugar
½   cup shredded white cheddar cheese (2 oz.)

1. In a large skillet cook bacon until crisp. Remove to paper towels to drain, reserving drippings. Crumble bacon and chill until needed. Reserve 2 Tbsp. bacon drippings; chill 1 hour or until firm (or omit drippings and use 2 Tbsp. additional shortening).
2. Preheat oven to 375°F. Line a baking sheet with parchment paper. For tart pastry, in a medium bowl combine flour and salt. Using a pastry blender, cut in shortening and chilled drippings until peasize. Sprinkle 1 Tbsp. of the water over part of the mixture; gently toss with a fork. Push the moistened flour mixture to side of bowl. Repeat moistening flour, gradually adding water until flour mixture begins to come together. Gather pastry into a ball, kneading gently just until it holds together.
3. On a lightly floured surface, use your hands to slightly flatten pastry. Roll pastry into a 13-inch circle. Transfer pastry to prepared baking sheet, being careful not to stretch pastry (pastry may hang over edges slightly).
4. In small saucepan melt apple jelly over medium heat. In a large bowl combine apple slices, half of the bacon, and the melted jelly. Spoon into the center of pastry, leaving a 2- to 3-inch border. Fold the pastry border up and over the filling, pleating the pastry to fit.
5. Brush the pastry with milk and sprinkle with sugar. Place tart on the center oven rack. Place a large baking sheet on the rack below the tart. Cover tart loosely with foil. Bake 15 minutes. Remove foil; bake 15 minutes more. Sprinkle filling with the remaining bacon and the cheese. Bake 10 to 15 minutes more or until pastry is golden and apples are tender. Cool 1 hour before serving. Store leftovers in the refrigerator. Makes 8 servings.
PER SERVING *294 cal., 16 g fat (5 g sat. fat), 14 mg chol., 195 mg sodium, 33 g carb., 1 g fiber, 6 g pro.*

BACON-CHEDDAR COUNTRY APPLE TART

MAPLE BREAD PUDDING WITH PECAN PRALINE

PREP 35 minutes
CHILL 1 hour
BAKE 40 minutes at 375°F
COOL 30 minutes

- 1 cup granulated sugar
- ¼ cup water
- ½ cup chopped pecans, toasted (tip, page 20)
- 8 eggs, lightly beaten
- 4 cups half-and-half or light cream
- 1 cup packed brown sugar
- 1 cup maple syrup
- 1 Tbsp. vanilla
- 1 lb. loaf egg bread, torn into bite-size pieces (about 14 cups)
  Vanilla ice cream (optional)

1. For pecan praline, lightly grease a baking sheet; set aside. In a small saucepan combine granulated sugar and the water. Cook over medium heat, stirring to dissolve sugar. Bring to boiling; reduce heat. Without stirring, boil gently, uncovered, 7 minutes or until mixture turns a deep amber color. Remove from heat. Stir in pecans. Quickly pour onto prepared baking sheet; cool. Break into pieces; set aside.

2. In an extra-large bowl combine eggs, half-and-half, brown sugar, maple syrup, and vanilla. Stir in bread pieces until moistened. Cover and chill 1 hour.

3. Preheat oven to 375°F. Lightly grease a 3-quart rectangular baking dish. Transfer bread mixture to baking dish. Bake 40 minutes or until top is golden and a knife inserted in center comes out clean.

4. Cool 30 minutes on a wire rack. Top with pecan praline. Serve warm with scoops of ice cream, if desired. Makes 12 servings.

PER SERVING 630 cal., 27 g fat (13 g sat. fat), 222 mg chol., 308 mg sodium, 87 g carb., 1 g fiber, 12 g pro.

MAPLE BREAD PUDDING WITH PECAN PRALINE

CHOCOLATE
CREPES WITH
NUTMEG VANILLA
SAUCE

CHOCOLATE CREPES WITH NUTMEG VANILLA SAUCE

PREP 30 minutes
CHILL 1 hour **STAND** 20 minutes
COOK 18 minutes

1	recipe Nutmeg Vanilla Sauce
1	cup all-purpose flour
⅓	cup sugar
⅓	cup unsweetened cocoa powder
2	eggs, lightly beaten
1	cup milk
2	Tbsp. butter, melted
1	tsp. vanilla
	Melted butter for cooking crepes
½	cup heavy cream
2	Tbsp. sugar
	Raspberries
	Chocolate curls

1. Prepare Nutmeg Vanilla Sauce.
2. In a small bowl stir together flour, ⅓ cup sugar, and cocoa powder. In a medium bowl whisk together eggs, milk, 2 Tbsp. butter, and vanilla; add flour mixture and whisk until combined. Let batter stand at room temperature 20 minutes.
3. Heat an 8-inch nonstick skillet over medium-high heat. Lightly brush skillet with melted butter. For each crepe, pour 3 Tbsp. of batter into center of skillet. Tip and swirl pan to get a thin even layer of batter. Cook 40 to 60 seconds. Using a rubber spatula loosen edge and flip crepe. Cook 10 seconds more. Invert pan over paper towels to remove crepe. Make 12 crepes total, adjusting heat and brushing skillet with butter as necessary.
4. In a chilled medium bowl combine heavy cream and 2 Tbsp. sugar. Beat with a mixer on medium until soft peaks form.
5. Fold each crepe in half then in quarters. Place two crepes each on six dessert plates. Drizzle with Nutmeg Vanilla Sauce; top with whipped cream, raspberries, and chocolate curls. Makes 6 servings.

Nutmeg Vanilla Sauce In a small saucepan stir together 3 egg yolks, ¾ cup milk, and 2 Tbsp. sugar. Cook and stir continuously over medium heat until sauce thickens and just coats the back of a clean metal spoon. Remove from heat. Stir in 1 tsp. vanilla and ⅛ tsp. nutmeg. Quickly cool sauce by placing the saucepan in a large bowl of ice water 1 to 2 minutes and stirring constantly.

COFFEE S'MORES TORTE

Pour sauce into a bowl. Cover surface with plastic wrap to prevent a skin from forming. Chill at least 1 hour, without stirring, before serving. Makes about 1 cup.
PER SERVING *371 cal., 18 g fat (10 g sat. fat), 219 mg chol., 92 mg sodium, 43 g carb., 1 g fiber, 10 g pro.*

COFFEE S'MORES TORTE

PREP 30 minutes
BAKE 10 minutes at 350°F
FREEZE 13 hours
BROIL 30 seconds

10	cinnamon graham cracker squares
⅔	cup sliced almonds, toasted (tip, page 20)
1	Tbsp. sugar
¼	cup butter, melted
1	qt. (4 cups) coffee ice cream, softened*
1	cup hot fudge-flavor ice cream topping
1	qt. (4 cups) dulce de leche ice cream, softened*
1	7-oz. jar marshmallow creme
2	cups tiny marshmallows
½	cup miniature semisweet chocolate pieces

1. Preheat oven to 350°F. For crust, in a food processor combine graham crackers, almonds, and sugar. Pulse until crackers are finely crushed. Add melted butter; pulse until crumbs are moistened. Press onto bottom of a 9-inch springform pan. Bake 10 to 12 minutes or until edges start to brown. Cool on a wire rack.
2. Using the back of a large spoon, spread coffee ice cream on crust. Spread fudge topping over ice cream. Freeze 1 hour or until topping is set.
3. Spread dulce de leche ice cream over fudge topping. Cover and freeze 12 to 24 hours.
4. Preheat broiler. Place springform pan on a baking sheet. Quickly spread marshmallow creme over top of torte. Sprinkle with marshmallows and chocolate pieces.
5. Broil about 4 inches from heat 30 to 60 seconds or just until marshmallows are golden. Using a warm knife, loosen torte from sides of pan; remove pan. Serve immediately. Makes 12 servings.
*Tip Place ice cream in a chilled bowl and stir with a wooden spoon until soft and smooth.
PER SERVING *538 cal., 24 g fat (12 g sat. fat), 37 mg chol., 255 mg sodium, 77 g carb., 2 g fiber, 6 g pro.*

WHITE CHOCOLATE CRÈME BRÛLÉE

on a wire rack. Cover and chill at least 1 hour or up to 8 hours.

5. Before serving, let custards stand at room temperature 20 minutes. Meanwhile, for caramelized sugar, in an 8-inch heavy skillet heat the 2 Tbsp. sugar over medium-high heat until sugar begins to melt, shaking skillet occasionally to heat sugar evenly. Do not stir. Once sugar starts to melt, reduce heat to low and cook 3 minutes or until all the sugar is melted and golden brown, stirring as needed with a wooden spoon.

6. Quickly drizzle caramelized sugar over custards. (If sugar hardens in the skillet, return to heat and stir until melted.) Serve immediately. Makes 6 servings.

PER SERVING *307 cal., 18 g fat (10 g sat. fat), 180 mg chol., 98 mg sodium, 31 g carb., 0 g fiber, 6 g pro.*

ALMOND PASTRY FINGERS

PREP 30 minutes
BAKE 20 minutes at 400°F
COOL 4 hours

- 1   17.3-oz. pkg. frozen puff pastry sheets, thawed (2 sheets)
- 1   12.5-oz. can almond pastry and dessert filling
- 1½ cups white baking pieces
- ⅔   cup slivered almonds, toasted (tip, page 20) and finely chopped
     Powdered sugar

1. Preheat oven to 400°F. Line an extra-large cookie sheet with parchment paper; set aside. Unfold pastry sheets onto a work surface. Cut each sheet lengthwise into two rectangles (four rectangles total). Using a fork, generously prick pastry.

2. Spread almond filling (about ¼ cup each) over pastry to within ¾ inch of edges. Top with white baking pieces and almonds. Brush pastry edges with water. Fold pastry in half lengthwise; gently press edges with fork to seal. Place pastry 2 inches apart on prepared cookie sheet.

3. Bake 20 to 25 minutes or until golden brown. Transfer pastry to a wire rack; cool at least 4 hours. Generously sprinkle with powdered sugar. Cut pastries crosswise into 12 pieces. Makes 48 servings.

PER SERVING *119 cal., 7 g fat (2 g sat. fat), 0 mg chol., 57 mg sodium, 13 g carb., 1 g fiber, 1 g pro.*

WHITE CHOCOLATE CRÈME BRÛLÉE

PREP 20 minutes
BAKE 30 minutes at 325°F
CHILL 1 hour
STAND 20 minutes

- 1¾ cups half-and-half
- 4   oz. white chocolate (with cocoa butter), chopped
- 5   egg yolks, lightly beaten
- ⅓   cup sugar
- 1   tsp. vanilla
- ⅛   tsp. salt
- 2   Tbsp. sugar

1. Preheat oven to 325°F. In a small heavy saucepan combine ½ cup of the half-and-half and the white chocolate; cook and stir over low heat just until chocolate is melted. Gradually whisk in remaining 1¼ cups half-and-half. Bring to simmering. Remove from heat.

2. Meanwhile, in a medium bowl whisk together egg yolks, the ⅓ cup sugar, vanilla, and salt just until combined. Slowly whisk hot white chocolate mixture into egg yolk mixture.

3. Place six 4-oz. ramekins or 6-oz. custard cups in a 3-quart rectangular baking dish. Evenly divide egg yolk-white chocolate mixture among ramekins or custard cups. Place baking dish on oven rack. Pour boiling water into baking dish to reach halfway up sides of ramekins or custard cups.

4. Bake 30 to 40 minutes or until a knife inserted near centers comes out clean (centers will shake slightly). Remove ramekins or custard cups from water; cool

ALMOND PASTRY
FINGERS

CHOCOLATE-
CRANBERRY
BISCOTTI, PAGE 102

ESPRESSO BALLS,
PAGE 96

PEPPERMINT
SNOWBALLS, PAGE 97

TROPICAL
THUMBPRINTS,
PAGE 96

Tempting Cookies & Bars

The words "Christmas" and "cookie" go together like a cold hand in a warm mitten. This time of year more than any other, bakers get busy making cookies for exchanges, as gifts for friends and neighbors, and, of course, to fill their own platters. Whether you want to drop, shape, roll and cut, or slice and bake, here are the perfect treats to sweeten the season.

BOURBON
CRANBERRY
CHIPPERS

BOURBON CRANBERRY CHIPPERS

PREP 30 minutes
STAND 1 hour 20 minutes
BAKE 8 minutes at 375°F
COOL 2 minutes

1	cup dried cranberries or cherries
¼	cup bourbon
1	cup butter, softened
1	cup packed brown sugar
½	cup granulated sugar
1	egg
1	tsp. vanilla
2½	cups all-purpose flour
1	cup regular rolled oats
1	tsp. baking soda
8	oz. semisweet chocolate, chopped
½	cup macadamia nuts, chopped
1	recipe Bourbon Ganache
	Flaked or coarse sea salt (optional)

1. Place cranberries and bourbon in a small bowl; cover and let stand 1 hour (do not drain).

2. Preheat oven to 375°F. Line cookie sheets with parchment paper; set aside. In a large bowl beat butter 30 seconds. Add sugars and beat until combined. Add egg and vanilla and beat until combined. Add flour, oats, and baking soda; beat until combined. Stir in the chocolate, nuts, and cranberry mixture. Shape into 1½-inch balls and arrange 2 inches apart on prepared cookie sheets. Using your thumb, make an indent in center of each ball. Bake 8 to 10 minutes or until lightly browned. Remove cookie sheet to wire rack. Use the rounded side of a teaspoon measure to repress indents and carefully press in edges, if necessary, to reshape cookies. Cool 2 minutes. Transfer cookies to wire rack to cool completely.

3. Fill each cookie center with Bourbon Ganache. Let stand until slightly firm or chill 10 to 15 minutes until firm. Sprinkle with salt, if desired. Makes 46 servings.

Bourbon Ganache Place 1 cup semisweet chocolate pieces in a small heatproof bowl; set aside. In a small saucepan bring 1 cup heavy cream just to simmering. Pour over chocolate; let stand 5 minutes. Stir until smooth. Stir in 1 Tbsp. bourbon and stir to combine. Let stand 15 minutes to thicken slightly.

PER SERVING *176 cal., 10 g fat (6 g sat. fat), 22 mg chol., 64 mg sodium, 21 g carb., 1 g fiber, 2 g pro.*

TROPICAL THUMBPRINTS

PREP 25 minutes
CHILL 1 hour
BAKE 10 minutes at 375°F

⅔ cup butter, softened
½ cup packed brown sugar
1 egg
½ tsp. coconut flavoring
1 tsp. lime zest
1½ cups all-purpose flour
1 cup macadamia nuts (optional)
½ cup lemon curd
Shredded coconut, toasted (tip, page 20) (optional)
Finely chopped macadamia nuts (optional)

1. In a large bowl beat butter with a mixer on medium to high 30 seconds. Add brown sugar. Beat until combined, scraping sides of bowl occasionally. Beat in egg, coconut flavoring, and lime zest until combined. Beat in as much flour as you can with mixer. Stir in any remaining flour. Cover and chill 1 hour or until easy to handle.
2. Preheat oven to 375°F. Grease cookie sheets; set aside. Shape dough into about thirty 1-inch balls. Place 1 inch apart on prepared cookie sheets. Press your thumb into center of each ball. Bake 10 to 12 minutes or until bottoms are light brown. If cookie centers puff during baking, repress with rounded side of a teaspoon measure. Transfer to a wire rack and cool completely. Just before serving, fill centers with lemon curd. If desired, sprinkle with coconut and/or finely chopped nuts. Makes 30 servings.
PER SERVING *93 cal., 5 g fat (3 g sat. fat), 21 mg chol., 44 mg sodium, 12 g carb., 1 g fiber, 1 g pro.*

CRANBERRY-FIG TASSIES

PREP 30 minutes
CHILL 1 hour
BAKE 30 minutes at 325°F
COOL 5 minutes

½ cup butter, softened
1 3-oz. pkg. cream cheese, softened
1 cup all-purpose flour
¼ cup finely chopped pecans
1 tsp. orange zest
½ cup orange juice

TROPICAL THUMBPRINTS

⅓ cup finely chopped dried Calimyrna figs
1 egg
¾ cup packed brown sugar
½ tsp. vanilla
Dash salt
¼ cup finely chopped cranberries
Sweetened whipped cream* or powdered sugar (optional)

1. In a large bowl beat butter and cream cheese with a mixer on medium to high 30 seconds. Stir in flour and pecans. Cover and chill dough 1 hour or until easy to handle.
2. Preheat oven to 325°F. Shape dough into 24 balls. Press each ball into bottoms and up the sides of 24 ungreased 1¾-inch muffin cups. Set aside.
3. In a small saucepan combine orange juice and figs. Bring just to boiling; remove from heat. Let stand 10 minutes to soften figs. Drain well; set figs aside.

4. In a medium bowl beat the egg with a fork. Stir in orange zest, brown sugar, vanilla, and salt. Stir in drained figs and cranberries. Spoon about 2 tsp. of the fig mixture into each dough-lined muffin cup. Do not overfill.
5. Bake 30 to 35 minutes or until edges are golden. Cool in pan on a wire rack 5 minutes. Carefully transfer tassies to a wire rack to cool. If desired, top cooled tassies with sweetened whipped cream or sprinkle with powdered sugar before serving. Makes 24 servings.
***** For sweetened whipped cream, in a medium bowl beat ½ cup heavy cream, 1 Tbsp. sugar, and ¼ tsp. vanilla with a mixer on medium just until soft peaks form (tips curl).
PER SERVING *114 cal., 6 g fat (3 g sat. fat), 23 mg chol., 50 mg sodium, 14 g carb., 1 g fiber, 1 g pro.*

CHOCOLATE CANNOLI

PREP 1 hour 30 minutes
CHILL 1 hour 30 minutes
COOK 1 minutes

2   15-oz. cartons ricotta cheese
½   cup granulated sugar
3   Tbsp. unsweetened cocoa powder
2   tsp. vanilla
1   tsp. orange zest
½   cup finely chopped dark or bittersweet chocolate
1   recipe Homemade Chocolate Cannoli or 18 purchased cannoli shells
    Powdered sugar (optional)

1. For filling, in a medium bowl combine first five ingredients (through orange zest) until nearly smooth. Fold in chopped chocolate. Cover and chill at least 30 minutes.
2. Meanwhile, prepare Homemade Chocolate Cannoli.
3. Spoon filling into a decorating bag fitted with a large open star or round tip. Pipe filling into cannoli shells. Cover and chill up to 1 hour. If desired, sprinkle lightly with powdered sugar before serving. Makes 18 servings.
Homemade Chocolate Cannoli In a medium bowl stir together 2 cups all-purpose flour, ½ cup sugar, ½ cup unsweetened cocoa powder, and ⅛ tsp. salt. Using a pastry blender, cut in ¼ cup shortening until mixture resembles coarse crumbs. In a small bowl combine 2 lightly beaten eggs, ¼ cup milk, and 2 Tbsp. honey. Stir into flour mixture just until dough forms a ball. Divide dough in half. Grease metal cannoli cylinders. Lightly beat one egg white. On a lightly floured pastry cloth or work surface, roll one portion of dough at a time into a 12-inch square. Cut square into nine 4-inch squares. Lightly wrap each diagonally around a prepared cylinder. Brush corner of dough with egg white; press to seal. Fry cannoli shells, a few at a time, in deep, hot vegetable oil (350°F) about 1 minute or until golden brown. Using tongs, carefully remove shells, draining any oil inside cylinders. Drain shells on paper towels; cool. Makes 18 cannoli.
PER SERVING *300 cal., 17 g fat (7 g sat. fat), 45 mg chol., 70 mg sodium, 30 g carb., 2 g fiber, 9 g pro.*

CHERRY-ALMOND SPRITZ SANDWICH COOKIES

PREP 20 minutes
BAKE 6 minutes at 350°F

1   cup granulated sugar
⅓   cup almond paste, crumbled
¾   cup butter, softened
¾   cup shortening
4   egg whites
1   tsp. vanilla
¼   tsp. salt
    Red paste food coloring
4   cups all-purpose flour
    Sanding sugar
1   recipe Cherry-Almond Filling

1. Preheat oven to 350°F. In a large bowl beat granulated sugar and almond paste with a mixer on medium to high until smooth. Add butter and shortening. Beat until fluffy, scraping sides of bowl occasionally. Bweat in egg whites, vanilla, and salt until combined. Gradually beat in enough food coloring until dough reaches desired shade of red. Beat in as much flour as you can with the mixer. Stir in any remaining flour.
2. Pack unchilled dough into a cookie press fitted with a ribbon plate. Force dough through cookie press into 2-inch-strips onto an ungreased cookie sheet, cutting dough from press with a small knife or metal spatula and spacing strips about 1 inch apart (about 104 strips). Sprinkle strips lightly with sanding sugar.
3. Bake 6 to 8 minutes or until edges are firm but not brown. Transfer cookies to a wire rack; cool.
4. Spread Almond-Cherry Filling on bottoms of half of cookies. Top with remaining cookies, bottom sides together. Makes 52 servings.
Cherry-Almond Filling Drain ¼ cup finely chopped maraschino cherries on paper towels; pat dry to remove any excess liquid. Set aside. In a medium mixing bowl beat 1 cup softened butter with a mixer on medium to high 30 seconds. Gradually beat in 2 cups powdered sugar until combined. Beat in 1 tsp. cherry liqueur and ¼ tsp. almond extract. Gently stir in maraschino cherries. Makes 2 cups.
PER SERVING *163 cal., 10 g fat (5 g sat. fat), 16 mg chol., 71 mg sodium, 18 g carb., 0 g fiber, 1 g pro.*

CHOCOLATY MELTING SNOWMEN

PREP 50 minutes
BAKE 9 minutes at 350°F

½   cup shortening
½   cup peanut butter
½   cup granulated sugar
½   cup packed brown sugar
¼   cup unsweetened cocoa powder
1   tsp. baking powder
¼   tsp. salt
⅛   tsp. baking soda
1   egg
3   Tbsp. milk
½   tsp. vanilla
1½ cups all-purpose flour
16 oz. vanilla-flavor candy coating, coarsely chopped
20 bite-size chocolate-covered peanut butter cups
    Miniature chocolate chips and orange sprinkles

1. Preheat oven to 350°F. In a large bowl beat shortening and peanut butter with a mixer on medium 30 seconds. Add sugars, cocoa powder, baking powder, salt, and baking soda. Beat until combined, scraping bowl as needed. Beat in egg, milk, and vanilla. Beat in flour.
2. Shape dough into 20 balls; place 2 inches apart on an ungreased cookie sheet.
3. Bake 9 to 11 minutes or just until edges are firm. Cool on cookie sheet 2 minutes. Remove; cool on a wire rack.
4. In a medium microwave-safe bowl heat candy coating on medium 2½ to 3 minutes or until melted and smooth, stirring every 30 seconds.
5. For snowmen, spoon melted coating onto cookies to resemble melting snow. While coating is tacky, add peanut butter cups for top hats, mini chocolate chips for eyes, and orange sprinkles for noses. Makes 20 servings.
PER SERVING *315 cal., 17 g fat (9 g sat. fat), 10 mg chol., 101 mg sodium, 38 g carb., 1 g fiber, 3 g pro.*

CHOCOLATY MELTING
SNOWMEN

ESPRESSO BALLS

PEPPERMINT SNOWBALLS

PREP 20 minutes
BAKE 9 minutes at 350°F
COOL 6 minutes

1   cup butter, softened
⅔   cup powdered sugar
½   cup crushed peppermint candies
     (about 20)
1   tsp. vanilla
½   tsp. salt
2   cups all-purpose flour
1   cup powdered sugar
     Very finely crushed peppermint
     candies (optional)

1. Preheat oven to 350°F. Line cookie sheets with parchment paper; set aside. In a large bowl beat butter with a mixer on medium to high 30 seconds. Add the ⅔ cup powdered sugar, ½ cup crushed peppermint candies, vanilla, and salt. Beat until combined, scraping sides of bowl occasionally. Beat in as much flour as you can with the mixer. Stir in any remaining flour.
2. Shape dough into 1-inch balls. Place balls 2 inches apart on prepared cookie sheets. Bake 9 to 11 minutes or until cookies are set and bottoms are light golden. Cool on cookie sheets 1 minute. Transfer to a wire rack; cool 5 minutes. Roll warm cookies in 1 cup powdered sugar. Cool cookies completely on wire rack. Roll cooled cookies in powdered sugar again. If desired, lightly dust cookies with very finely crushed peppermint candies. Makes 36 servings.
Make Ahead Dough may be shaped into balls, then frozen on parchment- or foil-lined cookie sheets. Transfer frozen balls to an airtight container; cover. Freeze up to 3 months. To bake, arrange frozen balls on cookie sheets. Let stand at room temperature while oven preheats. Bake 10 to 12 minutes or until set and light golden on bottoms.
PER SERVING *103 cal., 5 g fat (3 g sat. fat), 14 mg chol., 79 mg sodium, 14 g carb., 1 g pro.*

ESPRESSO BALLS

PREP 25 minutes
BAKE 15 minutes at 325°F
COOL 3 minutes

1   cup butter, softened
½   cup powdered sugar
¼   cup unsweetened cocoa powder
1   Tbsp. coffee liqueur
1   tsp. vanilla
1¾   cups all-purpose flour
1½   cups hazelnuts (filberts), toasted
      and ground*
¼   cup chocolate-covered coffee
      beans, ground
      Whole chocolate-covered coffee
      beans

1. Preheat oven to 325°F. In a large bowl beat butter with a mixer on medium to high 30 seconds. Add powdered sugar and cocoa powder; beat until combined. Beat in coffee liqueur and vanilla. Beat in as much flour as you can with the mixer. Stir in any remaining flour, ½ cup of the ground hazelnuts, and ground coffee beans.
2. Shape dough into 1-inch balls. Roll in remaining ground hazelnuts. Place balls 2 inches apart on ungreased cookie sheets.
3. Bake 15 minutes or until bottoms are light brown. Lightly press a whole coffee bean onto top of each cookie. Cool on cookie sheets on wire racks 3 minutes. Transfer cookies to wire racks; let cool. Makes 54 servings.
*Tip Spread hazelnuts in a single layer in a shallow baking pan. Bake in a 325°F oven 15 to 20 minutes or until light golden brown, stirring once or twice; cool completely. Remove papery skins by rubbing with a clean dish towel. Pulse nuts in a food processor until ground. Be careful not to overprocess.
PER SERVING *79 cal., 6 g fat (3 g sat. fat), 9 mg chol., 28 mg sodium, 6 g carb., 1 g pro.*

PEPPERMINT
SNOWBALLS

COCONUT-PECAN SANDIES

PREP 45 minutes
CHILL 30 minutes
BAKE 15 minutes at 325°F

- 1 cup butter, softened
- ½ cup powdered sugar
- 1 Tbsp. water
- 1 tsp. vanilla
- 2 cups all-purpose flour
- ¾ cup finely chopped pecans, toasted (tip, page 20)
- ¾ cup finely chopped coconut
- ¾ cup powdered sugar

1. In a large bowl beat butter with a mixer on medium to high 30 seconds. Add the ½ cup powdered sugar. Beat until combined, scraping sides of bowl occasionally. Beat in the water and vanilla until combined. Beat in as much flour as you can with the mixer. Stir in any remaining flour, pecans, and coconut. Cover and chill 30 minutes or until dough is easy to handle.

2. Preheat oven to 325°F. Shape dough into about thirty-six 1-inch balls or 2×½-inch logs. Place 1 inch apart on ungreased cookie sheet. Bake 15 minutes or until bottoms are light brown. Transfer cookies to a wire rack to cool.

3. Place the ¾ cup powdered sugar in a large plastic bag. Add cooled cookies, a few at a time, shaking gently to coat. Makes 36 servings.

PER SERVING *99 cal., 7 g fat (3 g sat. fat), 12 mg chol., 45 mg sodium, 10 g carb., 1 g fiber, 1 g pro.*

MACADAMIA MOONS WITH BROWNED BUTTER GLAZE

PREP 50 minutes
BAKE 10 minutes at 350°F

- 1 cup butter, softened
- ⅔ cup granulated sugar
- ¾ tsp. ground ginger
- ½ tsp. vanilla
- 2¼ cups all-purpose flour
- 1 cup finely chopped macadamia nuts
- ¼ cup butter
- 2 cups powdered sugar
- 2 to 3 Tbsp. milk
- ¼ tsp. ground ginger
- ½ cup finely chopped macadamia nuts
  Grated whole nutmeg (optional)

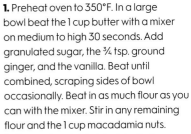

1. Preheat oven to 350°F. In a large bowl beat the 1 cup butter with a mixer on medium to high 30 seconds. Add granulated sugar, the ¾ tsp. ground ginger, and the vanilla. Beat until combined, scraping sides of bowl occasionally. Beat in as much flour as you can with the mixer. Stir in any remaining flour and the 1 cup macadamia nuts.

2. Shape dough into 1-inch balls. For moons, roll balls into short logs with tapered ends. Place logs 1 inch apart on ungreased cookie sheet. Curve logs slightly into crescents. Bake 10 to 11 minutes or until set but not brown. Transfer cookies to a wire rack; cool.

3. For browned butter, in a small heavy saucepan stir the ¼ cup butter over medium heat until melted. Continue cooking 6 to 9 minutes or until butter turns golden, stirring frequently. Cool slightly.

4. For glaze, in a bowl stir together browned butter, powdered sugar, 2 Tbsp. of the milk, and the ¼ tsp. ground ginger. Stir in enough remaining milk, 1 tsp. at a time, to reach drizzling consistency.

5. Drizzle cookies with glaze. Sprinkle with the ½ cup macadamia nuts and, if desired, grated nutmeg. Makes 48 servings.

PER SERVING *125 cal., 8 g fat (4 g sat. fat), 13 mg chol., 43 mg sodium, 13 g carb., 1 g fiber, 1 g pro.*

COCONUT-PECAN SANDIES

CHOCOLATE
PALMIERS

CHOCOLATE PALMIERS

PREP 40 minutes
CHILL 4 hours
BAKE 8 minutes at 375°F

- 1   8-oz. pkg. cream cheese, softened
- ½   cup powdered sugar
- ¼   cup unsweetened cocoa powder
- 2   Tbsp. all-purpose flour
- 2   Tbsp. coffee liqueur or brewed coffee
- ½   cup finely chopped, toasted pecans or hazelnuts (filberts) (tip, page 20) (optional)
- ½   cup butter, softened
- ½   cup granulated sugar
- ½   cup packed brown sugar
- ½   tsp. baking powder
- ½   tsp. ground cinnamon
- ¼   tsp. salt
- 1   egg
- 3   Tbsp. milk
- ½   tsp. vanilla
- 2¾   cups all-purpose flour

1. For filling, in a bowl beat the first five ingredients (through liqueur) with a mixer on low to medium until smooth. If desired, stir in nuts. Cover and set aside.
2. In a large bowl beat butter on medium to high 30 seconds. Add granulated sugar, brown sugar, baking powder, cinnamon, and salt. Beat until combined, scraping sides of bowl occasionally. Beat in egg, milk, and vanilla until combined. Beat in as much flour as you can with the mixer. Stir in any remaining flour. Divide dough in half. If necessary, cover and chill dough 30 minutes or until easy to handle.
3. On a lightly floured surface, roll half the dough into a 12×8-inch rectangle. Spread half the filling over dough rectangle to within ½ inch of each long edge. Roll long edges toward center scroll fashion. Brush water on seam where dough spirals meet; lightly press together. Repeat with remaining dough and filling. Wrap each roll in plastic wrap. Chill 4 hours or until dough is firm enough to slice.

4. Preheat oven to 375°F. Grease a large cookie sheet; set aside. Using a sharp thin-blade knife, cut each roll into about thirty-six ¼-inch slices. Place slices 2 inches apart on prepared cookie sheet. Bake 8 minutes or until edges are firm and bottoms are lightly browned. Transfer cookies to a wire rack to cool. Makes 36 servings.
PER SERVING 117 cal., 5 g fat (3 g sat. fat), 19 mg chol., 70 mg sodium, 16 g carb., 2 g pro.
Quick Puff Pastry Palmiers Cut a few steps by swapping homemade dough for two sheets thawed frozen puff pastry. Roll each sheet of pastry into a 12×9-inch rectangle. Fill, roll, chill, and slice as directed. Bake 12 to 14 minutes at 400°F or until edges are browned and crisp.

SOUR CREAM AND
CHERRY PINWHEELS

SOUR CREAM AND CHERRY PINWHEELS

PREP 40 minutes
CHILL 2 hours
BAKE 8 minutes at 375°F
COOL 3 minutes

½ cup butter, softened
1 cup granulated sugar
1 tsp. baking powder
¼ tsp. baking soda
Dash salt
1 egg
½ cup sour cream
1 tsp. lemon zest
1 tsp. vanilla
2¾ cups all-purpose flour
¾ cup cherry preserves
1 cup powdered sugar
3 to 4 tsp. milk
¼ tsp. almond extract

1. In a large bowl beat butter with a mixer on medium to high 30 seconds. Add granulated sugar, baking powder, baking soda, and salt. Beat until combined, scraping sides of bowl occasionally. Beat in egg, sour cream, lemon zest, and vanilla until combined. Beat in as much flour as you can with the mixer. Stir in any remaining flour. Divide dough into four portions. Cover and chill 2 hours or until easy to handle.

2. Preheat oven to 375°F. Line a cookie sheet with parchment paper. On a lightly floured surface, roll one portion of dough at a time into a 7½-inch square. Using a straight or fluted pastry wheel, cut each dough square into about nine 2½-inch squares. (Keep remaining dough chilled until needed. If dough becomes too soft, return it to refrigerator for a few minutes.)

3. Place squares 2 inches apart on prepared cookie sheet. Using the pastry wheel, cut 1-inch slits from corners toward center of each square. Snip any large pieces of fruit in preserves. Spoon 1 level tsp. preserves into center of each square. Fold every other tip (one from each corner) into the center of each square to form a pinwheel shape. Press dough gently in center to seal tips to filling.

4. Bake 8 to 9 minutes or just until edges begin to brown. Cool on cookie sheet 3 minutes. Transfer cookies to a wire rack to cool.

5. For icing, in a bowl stir together powdered sugar, 1 Tbsp. of the milk, and almond extract. If necessary, stir in enough remaining milk to reach drizzling consistency. Drizzle cookies with icing. Let stand until icing is set. Makes 36 servings.
PER SERVING *118 cal., 3 g fat (2 g sat. fat), 13 mg chol., 52 mg sodium, 21 g carb., 0 g fiber, 1 g pro.*

LEMONY SNOWFLAKE SANDWICHES

PREP 45 minutes
CHILL 2 hours
BAKE 7 minutes at 375°F
COOL 1 minute

½ cup butter, softened
½ cup butter-flavor shortening
1 cup granulated sugar
2 tsp. lemon zest
¾ tsp. baking powder
¼ tsp. baking soda
Dash salt
1 egg
⅓ cup sour cream
1 tsp. vanilla
2¾ cups all-purpose flour
1 recipe Creamy Lemon Filling
Powdered sugar

1. In a large bowl beat butter and shortening with a mixer on medium 30 seconds. Add sugar, lemon zest, baking powder, baking soda, and salt. Beat until combined, scraping bowl as needed. Beat in egg, sour cream, and vanilla. Beat in flour. Divide dough in half. Cover and chill 2 hours or until easy to handle.

2. Preheat oven to 375°F. On a lightly floured surface, roll one portion of dough at a time to ⅛-inch thickness. Using a 2½- to 3-inch snowflake-shape cookie cutter, cut out dough. Using a 1-inch diamond- or circle-shape cookie cutter, cut and remove a shape from center half of the cookies. Place cutouts 1 inch apart on an ungreased cookie sheet.

3. Bake 7 to 8 minutes or until edges are firm and bottoms are very light brown. Cool on cookie sheet 1 minute. Remove; cool on a wire rack.

4. Spread Creamy Lemon Filling on bottoms of cookies without cutout centers. Top with cookies with cutout centers, bottom sides down. Sprinkle generously with powdered sugar. Makes 40 servings.

LEMONY SNOWFLAKE SANDWICHES

Creamy Lemon Filling In a small bowl beat ⅓ cup mascarpone cheese or 3 oz. softened cream cheese and 1 Tbsp. softened butter with a mixer on medium 30 seconds. Beat in ¼ cup lemon curd. Gradually beat in 1 cup powdered sugar.
PER SERVING *129 cal., 7 g fat (3 g sat. fat), 17 mg chol., 47 mg sodium, 16 g carb., 0 g fiber, 2 g pro.*
To Store Layer unfilled cookies between sheets of waxed paper in an airtight container. Store at room temperature up to 3 days or freeze up to 3 months. To serve, thaw cookies if frozen. Fill as directed.

CHOCOLATE-CRANBERRY BISCOTTI

PREP 35 minutes
BAKE 20 minutes at 375°F + 15 minutes at 325°F
COOL 1 hour

½ cup butter, softened
⅔ cup sugar
⅓ cup unsweetened cocoa powder
2 tsp. baking powder
2 eggs
2 cups all-purpose flour
½ cup semisweet chocolate pieces
½ cup dried cranberries or dried cherries
1 cup powdered sugar
3 Tbsp. cocoa powder
¼ tsp. vanilla
1 tsp. milk

1. Preheat oven to 375°F. Lightly grease a large cookie sheet; set aside. In a large bowl beat butter with a mixer 30 seconds. Add sugar, the ⅓ cup cocoa powder, and baking powder. Beat until combined, scraping sides of bowl occasionally. Beat in eggs until combined. Beat in as much flour as you can with mixer. Stir in any remaining flour. Stir in chocolate pieces and dried cranberries.
2. Divide dough in half. Shape each portion into a 9-inch-long roll. Place rolls 5 inches apart on prepared cookie sheet; flatten to about 2 inches wide.
3. Bake 20 minutes or until a wooden toothpick inserted near center comes out clean. Cool on cookie sheet 1 hour. (For easy slicing, wrap cooled rolls in plastic wrap and let stand overnight at room temperature.)
4. Preheat oven to 325°F. Use a serrated knife to diagonally cut each roll into ½-inch slices (about 28 slices). Place slices, cut sides down, on an ungreased cookie sheet. Bake 8 minutes. Turn slices over and bake 7 to 9 minutes or until dry and crisp. (If baking slices after cooling logs only

1 hour, increase bake time 1 to 2 minutes per side.) Transfer to a wire rack to cool.
5. For drizzle, in a bowl stir together powdered sugar, 3 Tbsp. cocoa powder, and vanilla. Stir in milk, ½ tsp. at a time, until icing is drizzling consistency. Makes 28 servings.
PER SERVING *109 cal., 5 g fat (3 g sat. fat), 24 mg chol., 55 mg sodium, 16 g carb., 1 g fiber, 2 g pro.*

SUGAR COOKIE CUTOUTS

PREP 40 minutes
CHILL 30 minutes
BAKE 7 minutes at 375°F

1 cup butter, softened
1¼ cups granulated sugar
1½ tsp. baking powder
½ tsp. salt
2 eggs
2 tsp. vanilla
3 cups all-purpose flour
1 recipe Creamy White Frosting (recipe, page 79) (optional)
1 recipe Powdered Sugar Icing (optional)
Assorted decorations (optional)

1. In a large mixing bowl beat butter on medium to high 30 seconds. Add granulated sugar, baking powder, and salt. Beat until combined, scraping sides of bowl occasionally. Beat in eggs and vanilla until combined. Beat in as much flour as you can with mixer. Stir in any remaining flour. Divide dough in half. Cover and chill dough 30 minutes or until easy to handle.
2. Preheat oven to 375°F. On a floured surface, roll half the dough at a time to ⅛- to ¼-inch thickness. Using 2½-inch cookie cutters, cut into shapes. Place 1 inch apart on ungreased cookie sheets.
3. Bake 7 minutes or until edges are firm and bottoms are very light brown. Transfer cookies to wire racks to cool. If desired, frost with Creamy White Frosting or Powdered Sugar Icing and decorate. Makes about 52 servings.
PER SERVING *80 cal., 4 g fat (2 g sat. fat), 17 mg chol., 63 mg sodium, 10 g carb., 0 g fiber, 1 g pro.*
Powdered Sugar Icing Stir together 1 cup powdered sugar, 1 Tbsp. milk, and ¼ tsp. vanilla. Stir in additional milk, 1 tsp. at a time, until spreading consistency.

CHOCOLATE-CRANBERRY BISCOTTI

SCANDINAVIAN
BROWNIES

SCANDINAVIAN BROWNIES

PREP 20 minutes
BAKE 30 minutes at 350°F

    Nonstick cooking spray
4   oz. unsweetened chocolate,
    coarsely chopped
⅔   cup butter, cut in pieces
3   Tbsp. water
¾   cup granulated sugar
¾   cup packed brown sugar
3   eggs
1   tsp. vanilla
1   cup all-purpose flour
¾   cup whole almonds, toasted and
    ground*
½   tsp. ground cardamom
¼   tsp. salt
    Powdered sugar (optional)

1. Preheat oven to 350°F. Line an
8×8×2-inch baking pan with foil,
extending foil 1 inch over edges. Coat with
cooking spray. In a large microwave-safe
bowl combine chocolate, butter, and the
water. Microwave, uncovered, on high
1 minute, stirring after 30 seconds.
Remove and stir until smooth.
2. Add granulated sugar and brown
sugar; stir to combine. Add eggs and
vanilla; stir to combine. Stir in flour, ground
almonds, cardamom, and salt until
smooth. Spoon batter into prepared pan.
3. Bake 30 minutes or until edges are set
and start to pull away from sides of pan.
Cool in pan on a wire rack. Use foil to lift
from pan; remove foil. If desired, lay a
snowflake stencil on top. Sift powdered
sugar over stencil. Cut into bars. Makes
16 servings.
*Tip Place nuts in a shallow baking pan.
Bake in a 350° oven 5 to 10 minutes or
until lightly toasted, stirring once or twice.
Cool. In a food processor, pulse nuts until
ground; be careful not to overprocess.
PER SERVING *175 cal., 10 g fat (5 g sat. fat),
37 mg chol., 82 mg sodium, 20 g carb.,
1 g fiber, 3 g pro.*

GINGERBREAD STARS

PREP 40 minutes
CHILL 3 hours
BAKE 5 minutes at 375°F
STAND 1 hour

3   cups all-purpose flour
2   tsp. ground ginger
1   tsp. baking soda

GINGERBREAD STARS

½   tsp. salt
½   tsp. ground cinnamon
½   tsp. ground cloves
½   cup butter, softened
¼   cup shortening
¾   cup sugar
½   cup molasses
1   egg
1   recipe Powdered Sugar Icing
    (recipe, page 102)
    Silver and gold coarse sugars

1. In a medium bowl stir together the first
six ingredients (through cloves). Set aside.
2. In a large bowl beat butter and
shortening with a mixer on medium
to high 30 seconds. Add sugar and
molasses; beat until combined. Add egg;
beat well. Add flour mixture; beat on
low just until combined. Divide dough in
half. Cover and chill 3 hours or until easy
to handle.

3. Preheat oven to 375°F. On a well-
floured surface, roll half the dough at
a time to ⅛-inch thickness. Using 3- to
4-inch star-shape cookie cutters, cut
shapes. Place 1 inch apart on lightly
greased cookie sheets.
4. Bake 5 to 7 minutes or until edges are
very lightly browned. Cool on cookie
sheet 1 minute. Remove cookies and cool
completely on a wire rack.
5. Spread Powdered Sugar Icing on
cookies and decorate as desired with
silver and gold sugars. Let stand 1 hour or
until icing is set. Makes 26 servings.
PER SERVING *176 cal., 6 g fat (3 g sat. fat),
17 mg chol., 130 mg sodium, 29 g carb.,
2 g pro.*

LEMON BLONDIES

BERRY BLONDIES

PREP 30 minutes
BAKE 25 minutes at 350°F

2   cups packed brown sugar
⅔   cup butter
2   cups whole almonds, toasted (tip, page 20)
1   tsp. almond extract
1   tsp. vanilla
2   eggs
2   cups all-purpose flour
1½ tsp. baking powder
1   cup dried cranberries

1. Preheat oven to 350°F. Line a 13×9-inch baking pan with foil, extending foil over edges of pan. Grease foil; set pan aside.
2. In a large saucepan stir brown sugar and butter over medium heat until butter is melted and mixture is smooth. Remove from heat.
3. Coarsely chop 1 cup of the almonds; set aside. Place remaining 1 cup almonds in a food processor. Cover and process until a paste begins to form. Stir almond paste, almond extract, and vanilla into butter mixture. Stir in eggs, one at a time, until combined. In a bowl stir together flour and baking powder; gradually stir flour mixture into butter mixture until combined. Stir in chopped almonds and dried cranberries.
4. Pour batter into prepared baking pan, spreading evenly. Bake 25 minutes. Cool in pan on a wire rack. Using edges of foil, lift uncut bars from pan. Cut into bars. Makes 32 servings.
PER SERVINGS *183 cal., 9 g fat (3 g sat. fat), 22 mg chol., 65 mg sodium, 25 g carb., 2 g fiber, 3 g pro.*

SALTED CARAMEL, CHOCOLATE, AND PEANUT CRACKER-STACK BARS

PREP 30 minutes
CHILL 2 hours

8   oz. rich rectangular crackers (such as Club crackers)
¾   cup butter (1½ sticks)
¾   cup honey
1   cup packed brown sugar
⅓   cup heavy cream
2   cups finely crushed graham crackers
1   tsp. vanilla

LEMON BLONDIES

PREP 30 minutes
BAKE 30 minutes at 325°F

1½ cups all-purpose flour
1   tsp. baking powder
¼   tsp. salt
½   cup butter, softened
¾   cup packed brown sugar
½   cup granulated sugar
2   eggs
2   tsp. vanilla
½   cup chopped macadamia nuts, toasted (tip, page 30)
1   10-oz. jar lemon curd

1. Preheat oven to 325°F. Line a 9×9×2-inch baking pan with foil, extending foil over edges of pan. Grease foil; set pan aside.
2. In a medium bowl stir together flour, baking powder, and salt. In a large bowl beat butter with a mixer on medium to high 30 seconds. Add brown sugar and granulated sugar. Beat 5 minutes, scraping bowl occasionally. Add eggs, one at a time, beating well after each addition. Beat in vanilla. Gradually add flour mixture; beat on low until combined. Stir in ⅓ cup of the macadamia nuts.
3. Spread one-third of the batter in prepared baking pan. Drop large spoonfuls of lemon curd onto batter at 1-inch intervals. Top with remaining batter. Gently swirl a knife through batter and lemon curd layers to marble. Sprinkle with remaining macadamia nuts.
4. Bake 30 minutes or until golden and set. Cool in pan on a wire rack. Using edges of foil, lift out of pan. Cut into bars. Makes 20 servings.
PER SERVING *204 cal., 8 g fat (4 g sat. fat), 41 mg chol., 122 mg sodium, 32 g carb., 2 g fiber, 2 g pro.*

SALTED CARAMEL, CHOCOLATE, AND PEANUT CRACKER-STACK BARS

½   tsp. fine sea salt
2   cups chocolate-covered peanut butter cups, chopped into ½-inch pieces (9 oz.)
2   cups dry-roasted peanuts
1½ cups milk chocolate pieces (9 oz.)
⅓   cup butterscotch-flavor pieces
⅓   cup peanut butter

1. Line a 13×9-inch baking pan with nonstick foil, extending foil over edges of pan. Arrange half the crackers in a single layer on bottom of prepared pan. In a medium saucepan combine butter, honey, brown sugar, and cream. Bring to boiling, stirring constantly. Add graham cracker crumbs, reduce heat to a simmer and cook 5 minutes, stirring constantly. Remove from heat; stir in vanilla and ¼ tsp. of the sea salt.

2. Pour half the caramel mixture over crackers in prepared pan; spread to cover. Sprinkle with chopped peanut butter cups and peanuts. Pour remaining caramel on top. Arrange remaining crackers in a single layer over caramel, pressing slightly to secure.

3. For topping, in a medium microwave-safe bowl, combine chocolate and butterscotch pieces. Heat on high 2 to 3 minutes or until melted, stirring every 30 seconds. Stir in peanut butter until smooth. Spread chocolate mixture over cracker layer; immediately sprinkle with remaining ¼ tsp. sea salt.

4. Chill bars 2 hours or until completely firm. Using edges of the foil, lift uncut bars out of pan. Makes 32 servings.
PER SERVING 346 cal., 20 g fat (9 g sat. fat), 19 mg chol., 220 mg sodium, 38 g carb., 2 g fiber, 5 g pro.

CHOCOLATE-GLAZED CEREAL BARS

PREP 30 minutes
STAND 20 minutes

1   cup sugar
1   cup light-color corn syrup
1½   cups peanut butter
6   cups crisp rice cereal
1   cup tiny marshmallows
1   11.5-oz. pkg. milk chocolate pieces, melted

Premade icing decorations (Wilton or Fancy Flours) (optional)

1. Line a 13×9-inch baking pan with foil, extending foil over edges. Butter foil.
2. In a large heavy saucepan bring sugar and corn syrup just to boiling, stirring to dissolve sugar. Remove from heat. Stir in peanut butter until melted. Gently stir in cereal and marshmallows.
3. Transfer mixture to prepared pan; use buttered waxed paper to press firmly. Spread melted chocolate over cereal mixture. Let stand 20 minutes or until set. Using foil, lift out of pan. Cut into bars. If desired, decorate with a premade icing decoration. Makes 24 servings.
PER SERVING *298 cal., 14 g fat (5 g sat. fat), 6 mg chol., 133 mg sodium, 43 g carb., 2 g fiber, 6 g pro.*

SALTED CHOCOLATE CHIP COOKIE STICKS

PREP 35 minutes
BAKE 22 minutes at 375°F + 10 minutes at 325°F
COOL 1 hour

1   cup butter, softened
1½   cups packed brown sugar
¾   tsp. salt
½   tsp. baking soda
2   eggs
2   tsp. vanilla
2¾   cups all-purpose flour
2   cups coarsely chopped semisweet or bittersweet chocolate
      Sea salt flakes

1. Preheat oven to 375°F. Line a 13×9-inch baking pan with foil, extending foil over edges.
2. In a large bowl beat butter with a mixer on medium 30 seconds. Add brown sugar, ¾ teaspoon salt, and baking soda. Beat until combined, scraping bowl as needed. Beat in eggs and vanilla. Beat in flour. Stir in chocolate. Press dough into prepared pan. If desired, sprinkle lightly with sea salt.
3. Bake 22 to 25 minutes or until light brown and center is set. Cool in pan on wire rack 1 hour.
4. Preheat oven to 325°F. Using foil, lift cookies out of pan. Cut in half lengthwise; cut crosswise into ½- to ¾-inch slices. Place, cut sides down, on a large ungreased cookie sheet. Bake 10 to 12 minutes or until cut edges are dry. Carefully remove; cool on wire racks. Makes 36 servings.
PER SERVING *166 cal., 8 g fat (5 g sat. fat), 24 mg chol., 178 mg sodium, 23 g carb., 1 g fiber, 2 g pro.*

CHOCOLATE-GLAZED CEREAL BARS

SALTED CHOCOLATE
CHIP COOKIE STICKS

CHOCOLATE CHIP
COOKIE DOUGH
TRUFFLES,
PAGE 114

Foolproof Candies

You don't have to go to a candy shop for delicious and eye-catching Christmas confections. These easy recipes for toffee, truffles, meringues, caramels, and bark yield results that look and taste like they were made by a pro.

CHERRY-
CASHEW BARK,
PAGE 117

MARCONA
ALMOND
TOFFEE

MARCONA ALMOND TOFFEE

PREP 15 minutes
COOK 20 minutes
CHILL 30 minutes

Nonstick cooking spray
2 cups butter
2 cups sugar
1 tsp. salt
1 tsp. vanilla
1 cup chopped white baking chocolate (6 oz.)
1 tsp. shortening
1 cup roasted and salted Marcona almonds

1. Line a 15×10×1-inch baking pan with foil; coat foil with nonstick cooking spray and set aside.

2. In a large saucepan combine butter, sugar, and salt. Stir over medium heat until sugar has completely melted and mixture boils. Clip a candy thermometer to pan and continue stirring over medium heat until mixture reaches 290°F, about 15 minutes. Remove from heat and stir in vanilla.

3. Pour into prepared pan, tipping pan to spread evenly. Allow to cool on a wire rack. In a small saucepan melt white baking chocolate with the shortening. Spread over toffee and sprinkle with almonds. Chill 30 minutes or until chocolate is set. Break into pieces. Makes 24 servings.

PER SERVING *276 cal., 21 g fat (11 g sat. fat), 42 mg chol., 238 mg sodium, 22 g carb., 1 g fiber, 2 g pro.*

CHOCOLATE CHIP MERINGUES

PREP 25 minutes
BAKE 20 minutes at 300°F

Shortening
2 egg whites
½ tsp. vanilla
⅛ tsp. cream of tartar
⅔ cup sugar
⅔ cup miniature semisweet chocolate pieces
2 oz. semisweet chocolate, melted (optional)

1. Preheat oven to 300°F. Lightly grease a cookie sheet. For meringue, in a medium bowl beat egg whites, vanilla, and cream of tartar with a mixer on medium until soft peaks form (tips curl). Gradually add sugar, about 1 Tbsp. at a time, beating on high until stiff peaks form (tips stand straight). Fold in chocolate pieces.

2. Drop meringue by rounded teaspoons 2 inches apart onto prepared cookie sheet. Bake 20 minutes or until firm and bottoms are light brown. Cool on cookie sheet on a wire rack. If desired, drizzle with melted chocolate. Makes 36 servings.

PER SERVING *39 cal., 1 g fat (1 g sat. fat), 0 g chol., 3 mg sodium, 7 g carb., 0 g fiber, 0 g pro.*

To Store Layer cookies between sheets of waxed paper in an airtight container. Freeze up to 1 month.

CHOCOLATE CHIP MERINGUES

CHOCOLATE CHIP COOKIE DOUGH TRUFFLES

PREP 30 minutes
FREEZE 30 minutes
STAND 30 minutes

⅓ cup butter, softened
⅓ cup packed brown sugar
1 Tbsp. vanilla
1 cup all-purpose flour
1 cup miniature semisweet chocolate pieces
4 oz. dark or semisweet chocolate, chopped
4 oz. chocolate-flavor candy coating, chopped
1 Tbsp. shortening
 Multicolor nonpareils (optional)

1. Line a 15×10×1-inch baking pan with waxed paper; set aside. In a medium bowl beat butter, brown sugar, and vanilla with a mixer on medium until smooth. Beat in flour just until combined. Stir in semisweet chocolate pieces. Shape dough into thirty 1-inch balls (using a #60 scoop, if desired) and place in prepared baking pan. Cover and freeze 30 minutes or until firm.
2. Meanwhile, in a small saucepan heat dark chocolate, candy coating, and shortening over low heat until melted and smooth, stirring constantly. Remove from heat.
3. Line a tray or baking sheet with waxed paper. Using a fork, dip balls into melted chocolate, swirling to coat and allowing excess chocolate to drip back into saucepan. Place dipped balls on prepared tray. If desired, sprinkle with nonpareils. Let stand at room temperature or chill 30 minutes or until set. Makes 15 servings.

PER SERVING *182 cal., 10 g fat (6 g sat. fat), 8 mg chol., 29 mg sodium, 22 g carb., 1 g fiber, 2 g pro.*

NEAPOLITAN MARSHMALLOW TREATS

PREP 45 minutes
STAND 1 hour

6 Tbsp. butter
1 10-oz. pkg. tiny marshmallows
2 13-oz. jars marshmallow creme
1 tsp. vanilla
10 cups crisp rice cereal
½ cup miniature semisweet chocolate pieces
5 cups chocolate-flavor crisp rice cereal
2½ cups strawberry marshmallows (5 oz.)
1 Tbsp. strawberry jelly
4 to 6 drops red food coloring

1. Line a 13×9-inch baking pan with foil, extending foil over edges. Lightly butter foil. Set aside.
2. For vanilla layer, in a 4- to 6-quart Dutch oven melt 2 Tbsp. of the butter over low heat. Add 3 cups of the tiny marshmallows; stir until melted. Stir in 2 cups of the marshmallow creme and the vanilla. Remove from heat. Gently stir in 5 cups of the plain crisp rice cereal. Transfer to prepared pan; use buttered waxed paper to press firmly.
3. For chocolate layer, in same Dutch oven melt 2 Tbsp. of the butter over low heat. Add remaining tiny marshmallows; stir until melted. Stir in 2 cups of the marshmallow creme and the chocolate pieces. Remove from heat. Gently stir in chocolate cereal. Spoon onto vanilla layer; press firmly.
4. For strawberry layer, in same Dutch oven melt remaining 2 Tbsp. butter over low heat. Add strawberry marshmallows and jelly; stir until melted. Stir in remaining marshmallow creme and food coloring. Remove from heat. Gently stir in remaining 5 cups plain cereal. Spoon onto chocolate layer; press firmly.
5. To press layers together, cover top of bars with a sheet of waxed paper then a sheet of foil. Place another 13×9-inch baking pan on top of bars; add a few cans of food to top pan for weight. Let stand at least 1 hour. Using foil liner, lift bars out of pan. Use a buttered knife to cut into bars. Makes 24 servings.

PER SERVING *288 cal., 5 g fat (3 g sat. fat), 8 mg chol., 228 mg sodium, 60 g carb., 0 g fiber, 2 g pro.*

CHOCOLATE CHIP COOKIE DOUGH TRUFFLES

NEAPOLITAN
MARSHMALLOW
TREATS

DIPPED HOLIDAY
CARAMELS

DIPPED HOLIDAY CARAMELS

PREP 40 minutes
STAND 1 hour

- 12 oz. chocolate- and/or vanilla-flavor candy coating, coarsely chopped
- 1 cup almond toffee bits, crushed; finely chopped pistachio nuts; and/or nonpareils
- 1 14-oz. pkg. vanilla caramels, unwrapped

1. Line a large cookie sheet with waxed paper; set aside. Place candy coating in a 4-cup microwave-safe measure or bowl. Heat on high 2 minutes or just until coating is melted, stirring every 30 seconds.
2. Place toffee, nuts, and/or nonpareils in shallow dishes. If desired, insert a wooden toothpick or skewer into each caramel. Dip each caramel into melted candy coating, letting excess coating drip back into measure or bowl. (If not using toothpicks or skewers, drop caramel in coating, then use a fork to lift out caramel, drawing it across rim of measure or bowl to remove excess coating.) Place on prepared cookie sheet.
3. Drizzle additional melted chocolate(s) over the coated caramels, and/or sprinkle with toffee bits, nuts, or nonpareils. Let stand 1 hour or until coating is set. Makes 44 servings.

PER SERVING 92 cal., 4 g fat (3 g sat. fat), 1 mg chol., 54 mg sodium, 12 g carb. 0 g fiber, 0 g pro.

CHERRY-CASHEW BARK (PHOTO, PAGE 111)

PREP 20 minutes
CHILL 30 minutes

- 1 lb. vanilla-flavor candy coating, cut up
- 6 oz. white baking chocolate with cocoa butter, coarsely chopped
- 1½ cups snipped dried cherries
- 1 tsp. orange zest
- ½ cup chopped salted roasted cashews

1. Line a large cookie sheet with foil; set aside. In a medium heavy saucepan cook and stir candy coating and white chocolate over low heat until melted.

Remove from heat. Stir in 1 cup of the dried cherries and the orange zest.
2. Pour candy onto prepared cookie sheet. Spread in an even layer about ¼ inch thick. Sprinkle with remaining ½ cup dried cherries and cashews. Lightly press cherries and cashews into chocolate.
3. Chill 30 minutes or until firm. (Or let candy stand at room temperature several hours until firm.) Using edges of foil, lift candy from cookie sheet; carefully peel off foil and break or cut candy into pieces. Makes 48 servings.

PER SERVING 91 cal., 5 g fat (3 g sat. fat), 0 mg chol., 5 mg sodium, 13 g carb., 1 g fiber, 1 g pro.

Tropical Bark: Prepare as directed, except omit dried cherries, orange zest, and cashews. In a bowl combine 1 cup finely chopped toasted macadamia nuts, ½ cup toasted shredded coconut, ½ cup snipped dried pineapple, and 1 tsp. lime or lemon zest. Stir half the nut mixture into melted coating. Spread on cookie sheet as directed. Sprinkle with remaining nut mixture.

HAZELNUT HAYSTACKS

PREP 30 minutes
STAND 1 hour

- 8 oz. chocolate-flavor candy coating, chopped
- 4 oz. bittersweet chocolate, chopped
- ½ cup chocolate-hazelnut spread
- 2½ cups broken pretzel sticks
- 2½ cups chow mein noodles
- 1 cup chopped toasted hazelnuts Sea salt flakes (optional)

1. In a large saucepan combine candy coating, bittersweet chocolate, and hazelnut spread. Stir over low heat until melted and smooth. Stir in pretzel sticks, chow mein noodles, and hazelnuts.
2. Drop candy by heaping spoonfuls onto two large baking sheets lined with waxed paper or foil. If desired, sprinkle with salt. Let stand 1 hour or until chocolate is set. If necessary, refrigerate haystacks 30 minutes or until set. Store in a covered container in the refrigerator. Makes 54 servings.

PER SERVING 77 cal., 4 g fat (2 g sat. fat), 90 mg sodium, 9 g carb., 1 g fiber, 0 g chol., 1 g pro.

CARAMEL-POPCORN DROPS

START TO FINISH 30 minutes

- 6 cups popped popcorn
- 3 cups square pretzels or tiny pretzel twists
- 2 cups mixed nuts, coarsely chopped
- 1 cup golden raisins
- 1 20-oz. pkg. vanilla-flavor candy coating, coarsely chopped
- ⅔ cup caramel-flavor ice cream topping

1. Line an extra-large cookie sheet or tray with waxed paper; set aside. In an extra-large bowl combine popcorn, pretzels, mixed nuts, and raisins.
2. In a medium heavy saucepan stir candy coating over low heat until melted and smooth. Remove from heat. Stir in caramel topping.
3. Pour melted coating mixture over popcorn mixture. Stir gently to coat, slightly crushing pretzels. Drop by rounded tablespoons onto prepared cookie sheet. Let stand until set. Makes 48 servings.

PER SERVING 138 cal., 7 g fat (4 g sat. fat), 0 mg chol., 53 mg sodium, 18 g carb., 1 g fiber, 2 g pro.

CARAMEL-POPCORN DROPS

COFFEE BEAN MELTAWAYS

COFFEE BEAN MELTAWAYS

PREP 1 hour
CHILL 8 hours

3   oz. cream cheese, softened
2   Tbsp. butter, softened
1   Tbsp. instant espresso powder, dissolved in 1 tsp. hot water
1   Tbsp. unsweetened cocoa powder
4   cups powdered sugar

1. In a large bowl beat cream cheese and butter with a mixer until combined; beat in dissolved instant espresso powder and cocoa. Gradually beat in as much powdered sugar as you can; knead in remaining sugar.
2. Divide dough into four portions and loosely cover with plastic wrap to prevent drying. Roll one portion at a time into a 12-inch rope about ½-inch diameter; cut into ¼-inch slices with a sharp knife. Roll pieces into ovals and use a toothpick to make an indentation in center of each to resemble a coffee bean. Arrange on baking sheets lined with parchment paper. Cover with paper towels; chill 8 hours or overnight. Makes 160 servings.
PER SERVING *28 cal., 1 g fat (0 g sat. fat), 2 mg chol., 6 mg sodium, 6 g carb. 0 g fiber, 0 g pro.*

MEXICAN CHOCOLATE AND ESPRESSO CAKE POPS

PREP 1 hour
BAKE according to package directions
FREEZE 1 hour

1   pkg. 2-layer-size chocolate cake mix
1   recipe Mexican Chocolate Frosting
12 oz. chocolate- or vanilla-flavor candy coating, chopped
38 lollipop sticks
12 oz. semisweet, dark, or white baking chocolate, chopped
2   Tbsp. unsweetened cocoa
½   tsp. ancho chile powder

1. Prepare cake mix according to package directions for a 13×9-inch baking pan. Cool in pan on a wire rack. Line baking sheets with waxed paper.
2. Remove cooled cake from pan and crumble into an extra-large bowl. Add Mexican Chocolate Frosting. Beat with a mixer on low until combined. Using a small scoop, drop into about thirty-eight 1½-inch mounds onto prepared baking sheets; roll each mound into a ball. Freeze balls 30 minutes.
3. In a small microwave-safe dish heat 1 oz. of the candy coating on medium 1 minute or until melted and smooth, stirring once. Dip one end of each lollipop stick into melted coating then poke stick into a ball (coating adheres cake ball to stick). Freeze cake pops 30 to 60 minutes or until cake balls are firm.
4. In a small saucepan combine remaining candy coating and chopped chocolate. Heat over medium-low heat until mixture is melted and smooth, stirring frequently. Working in batches, dip cake balls into melted chocolate mixture. Allow excess to drip off. Poke ends of lollipop sticks into plastic foam or florist's foam to suspend pops until chocolate is set.
5. In a small bowl combine cocoa powder and chile powder; sift over pops before chocolate is set. After chocolate sets, transfer pops to airtight storage containers. Cover and refrigerate up to 1 week. Let stand at room temperature at least 30 minutes before serving. Makes 38 servings.
Mexican Chocolate Frosting In a small bowl stir together 2 Tbsp. milk, 1½ tsp. instant espresso coffee powder or instant coffee crystals, ½ tsp. vanilla, and ¼ tsp. ground cinnamon. In a small heavy saucepan melt 2 oz. Mexican chocolate, chopped, over medium-low heat, stirring constantly; remove from heat and set aside to cool slightly. In a medium bowl beat ¼ cup softened butter with a mixer on medium until smooth. Gradually add ¾ cup powdered sugar, beating well. Gradually add coffee mixture, beating until smooth. Beat in melted chocolate. Gradually beat in 2 cups powdered sugar. If needed, beat in enough additional milk, 1 tsp. at a time for spreading consistency.
PER SERVING *229 cal., 10 g fat (6 g sat. fat), 4 mg chol., 142 mg sodium, 36 g carb., 1 g fiber, 2 g pro.*

CHOCOLATE
PIZZELLE, PAGE 128

SAGE-OLIVE
BAGUETTES, PAGE 123

Beautifully Wrapped Food Gifts

For a christmas present that suits every taste, spend some time in the kitchen this season crafting homemade treats from this collection of cookies, candies, breads, and soup mix. Tasty food, prettily packaged, is always the perfect gift.

WASABI SHRIMP-
STUFFED BUNS

WASABI SHRIMP-STUFFED BUNS

PREP 35 minutes
STAND 20 minutes
RISE 15 minutes
BAKE 20 minutes at 375°F
COOL 10 minutes

1   16-oz. pkg. hot roll mix
⅔   cup tub-style cream cheese
    spread with chive and onion
½   cup chopped fresh pea pods
⅓   cup coarsely shredded carrot
1   to 1½ tsp. wasabi powder
8   oz. cooked peeled and deveined
    shrimp, chopped
1   egg
1   Tbsp. water
4   tsp. white and/or black sesame
    seeds

1. Prepare hot roll mix according to package directions through the kneading step. Cover dough and let rest 10 minutes. Divide dough into 16 portions; shape each portion into a ball. Cover and let rest 10 minutes.
2. Meanwhile, for filling, in a large bowl stir together cream cheese, pea pods, carrot, and wasabi powder; mix well. Fold in shrimp.
3. Grease a large baking sheet; set aside. On a lightly floured surface, roll dough portion to a 4½-inch circle. Place about 2 Tbsp. of the shrimp filling on each circle of dough. Bring edges of dough up around filling and pinch to seal.
4. Preheat oven to 375°F. Place buns, seam sides down, on prepared baking sheet. Cover and let rise 15 minutes. In a small bowl whisk together egg and the water; brush tops of buns. Sprinkle with sesame seeds.
5. Bake 20 to 25 minutes or until golden brown. Transfer to a wire rack to cool. Makes 16 servings.
PER SERVING *182 cal., 6 g fat (3 g sat. fat), 63 mg chol., 271 mg sodium, 23 g carb., 0 g fiber, 8 g pro.*

As a gift Paint outsides of the tins a solid color. Decorate sides and lids with assorted dot stickers. Using crafts glue, attach ribbon to edges of lid rims. Line tins with parchment paper or waxed paper, fill with buns or other treats, and cover.

SAGE-OLIVE BAGUETTES

PREP 35 minutes
RISE 1 hour 35 minutes
STAND 10 minutes
BAKE 30 minutes at 375°F

3½ to 4 cups bread flour or
    unbleached all-purpose flour
1   pkg. active dry yeast
¾   tsp. salt
1¼ cups warm water (120°F to 130°F)
½   cup coarsely chopped, pitted
    kalamata olives
2   to 3 Tbsp. snipped fresh sage or
    2 to 3 tsp. dried sage, crushed
1   egg white, lightly beaten
1   Tbsp. water

1. In a large mixing bowl stir together 1 cup of the flour, yeast, and salt. Add the 1¼ cups warm water. Beat on low to medium 30 seconds, scraping sides of bowl constantly. Beat on high 3 minutes. Stir in olives and sage. Stir in as much remaining flour as you can.
2. Turn dough out onto a lightly floured surface. Knead in enough remaining flour to make a stiff dough that is smooth and elastic (8 to 10 minutes). Shape dough into a ball. Place in a lightly greased bowl, turning once to grease surface of dough. Cover; let rise in a warm place until double in size (about 1 hour).
3. Punch dough down. Turn dough out onto a lightly floured surface. Divide in half; shape into balls. Cover; let rest 10 minutes. Meanwhile, lightly grease two baking sheets or two baguette pans; sprinkle lightly with flour.

4. Roll each dough half into a 14×5-inch rectangle. Starting from long sides, tightly roll up rectangles. Pinch seams to seal and slightly pull to taper ends. Place loaves, seam sides down, on prepared baking sheets. In a bowl stir together egg white and the 1 Tbsp. water; brush some on loaves. Let rise until nearly double in size (35 to 45 minutes).
5. Preheat oven to 375°F. Using a sharp knife, make three ¼-inch-deep diagonal cuts across each loaf. Bake 20 minutes. Brush again with egg white mixture. Bake 10 to 15 minutes or until bread sounds hollow when lightly tapped. Transfer to wire racks; cool. Makes 20 servings.
PER SERVING *94 cal., 1 g fat (0 g sat. fat), 0 mg chol., 129 mg sodium, 18 g carb., 1 g fiber, 3 g pro.*

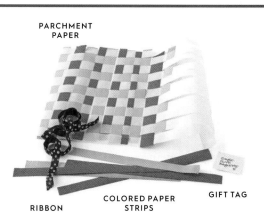

SAGE-OLIVE BAGUETTES

As a gift To weave a wrapper for a baguette, lay an 18-inch length of parchment paper flat. Mark 1 inch from each narrow edge. Then measure and mark 11 horizontal lines between marks on each edge. Cut along on each line, leaving edges intact. From pink and green paper, cut 1-inch strips, matching length to the width of the parchment. Weave the strips through the parchment. Wrap the baguette in plastic wrap, in the woven parchment, then tie with ribbons and a tag.

PARCHMENT PAPER

RIBBON   COLORED PAPER STRIPS   GIFT TAG

LONE-STAR CAVIAR SOUP MIX

PREP 15 minutes

3 Tbsp. reduced-sodium chicken bouillon granules
1 Tbsp. dried minced onion
1 Tbsp. dried parsley, crushed
1 tsp. dried oregano, crushed
1 tsp. ground ancho chile pepper
½ tsp. garlic powder
½ tsp. ground cumin
2 bay leaves
1 4-oz. container dried carrots, corn, peas, sweet peppers, and tomatoes*
1½ cups dried black-eyed peas and/or dried red kidney beans and/or dried black beans
Corn chips

1. For seasoning mix, in a small plastic bag combine the first eight ingredients (through bay leaves). Label and seal bag; set aside.
2. In a 1-quart glass jar layer the dried vegetable mixture. Place bag of seasoning mix on top. Place black-eyed peas in a small plastic bag; seal bag and place on top of seasoning mix. Fasten the lid. Include directions for making soup

Soup directions Remove and rinse dried black-eyed peas from jar. In a Dutch oven combine black-eyed peas and 4 cups water. Bring to boiling; reduce heat. Simmer, uncovered, 2 minutes. Remove from heat. Cover; let stand 1 hour. Drain and rinse. In the same Dutch oven combine soaked black-eyed peas, 7 cups fresh water, dried vegetable mix, and

LONE-STAR CAVIAR SOUP MIX

seasoning mix. Bring to boiling; reduce heat. Cover and simmer 2 hours or until beans are tender. Remove and discard bay leaves. If desired, serve soup with sour cream, corn chips, and/or shredded cheddar cheese. Makes 8 side-dish servings (8 cups soup).
*Tip Look for dried vegetables in the produce section of your supermarket.
PER SERVING 167 cal., 1 g fat (0 g sat. fat), 0 mg chol., 1,828 mg sodium, 34 g carb., 5 g fiber, 6 g pro.

CRANBERRY-WALNUT COOKIES

PREP 30 minutes
COOL 2 minutes
BAKE 10 minutes at 350°F

¾ cup butter, softened
1½ cups packed brown sugar
2 tsp. lemon zest
½ tsp. baking soda
½ tsp. baking powder
¼ tsp. salt
2 eggs
2 tsp. vanilla
2⅓ cups whole wheat flour
1½ cups chopped walnuts, toasted (tip, page 20)
1½ cups dried cranberries

1. Preheat oven to 350°F. In a large bowl beat butter with a mixer on medium to high 30 seconds. Add brown sugar, lemon zest, baking soda, baking powder, and salt. Beat until combined, scraping sides of bowl occasionally. Beat in eggs and vanilla. Beat in as much flour as you can with mixer. Stir in any remaining flour. Stir in walnuts and cranberries.
2. Drop dough by rounded teaspoons 2 inches apart onto ungreased cookie sheets. Bake 10 to 12 minutes or until edges are lightly brown. Cool on cookie sheets on wire racks 2 minutes. Transfer cookies to wire racks to cool completely. Makes 60 servings.
PER SERVING 86 cal., 5 g fat (2 g sat. fat), 12 mg chol., 47 mg sodium, 12 g carb., 1 g fiber, 1 g pro.

As a gift Individually wrap cookies in plastic wrap. Slide a coffee sleeve around each cookie and tie a ribbon around the sleeve.

1 QUART BAIL LID JAR

SCRAPBOOKING PAPER

RECIPE CARD

RIBBON

SNOWFLAKE STICKERS

As a gift From scrapbook paper cut a circle to fit glass top of jar; attach a snowflake sticker. Attach snowflake stickers to the ends of two ribbons. Attach circle to jar top and wrap ribbons around jar; secure with crafts glue. Tie a contrasting ribbon around jar and tuck in a recipe card with directions for making the soup.

CRANBERRY-
WALNUT COOKIES

COCONUT
MACAROONS

COCONUT MACAROONS

PREP 15 minutes
BAKE 20 minutes at 325°F
STAND 30 minutes

1   7-oz. pkg. flaked coconut
    (2⅔ cups)
⅔   cup sugar
⅓   cup all-purpose flour
¼   tsp. salt
3   egg whites, slightly beaten
½   tsp. almond extract
4   oz. chocolate-flavor candy
    coating, chopped (optional)

1. Preheat oven to 325°F. Line cookie sheets with parchment paper.
2. In a bowl stir together coconut, sugar, flour, and salt. Stir in egg whites and almond extract. Drop coconut mixture by teaspoons 1 inch apart onto prepared cookie sheets, making about thirty ¾- to 1-inch mounds.
3. Bake 20 minutes or until edges are golden. Cool cookies completely on cookie sheets. Carefully remove cookies from cookie sheets.
4. If desired, in a small heavy saucepan stir candy coating over low heat until melted. Dip bottoms of cooled cookies into melted candy coating, letting excess drip off. Place cookies, candy coating sides up, on parchment paper or waxed paper; let stand 30 minutes or until coating sets. Makes 30 cookies.
PER SERVING 73 cal., 4 g fat (4 g sat. fat), 0 mg chol., 57 mg sodium, 10 g carb., 1 g fiber, 1 g pro.

DOUBLE-CHOCOLATE CHIP COOKIES

PREP 30 minutes
BAKE 9 minutes at 350°F
COOL 2 minutes

½   cup butter, softened
½   cup shortening
1½ cups packed brown sugar
1   tsp. baking soda
½   tsp. salt
½   tsp. ground cinnamon
4   oz. semisweet chocolate, melted
    and cooled
2   eggs
2   tsp. vanilla
2½ cups all-purpose flour
6   oz. bittersweet chocolate, coarsely
    chopped
6   oz. semisweet chocolate, coarsely
    chopped
1   cup chopped pecans, toasted (tip,
    page 20)

1. Preheat oven to 350°F. In a large bowl beat butter and shortening with a mixer on medium 30 seconds. Add brown sugar, baking soda, salt, and cinnamon; beat until combined. Beat in cooled semisweet chocolate, eggs, and vanilla until combined. Beat in as much of the flour as you can with the mixer. Stir in any remaining flour, bittersweet chocolate, the chopped semisweet chocolate, and nuts.
2. Drop dough by heaping teaspoonfuls 2 inches apart onto ungreased cookie sheets. Bake 9 to 11 minutes or just until edges are set. Cool on cookie sheets

2 minutes. Transfer cookies to wire racks; cool. Makes 72 servings.
PER SERVING 101 cal., 6 g fat (3 g sat. fat), 9 mg chol., 46 mg sodium, 12 g carb., 1 g fiber, 1 g pro.

DOUBLE-CHOCOLATE CHIP COOKIES

TIN WITH WINDOW LID

PLEATED SCRAPBOOKING PAPER

IVY ADORNMENTS AND BUTTON

As a gift Adhere scrapbook paper around a square tin lid using crafts glue. Cut pleated scrapbooking paper to the diameter of tin box and glue it to side of tin. Attach ivy leaf scrapbooking adornments and a small button to the pleated paper.

As a gift Cut away one side of a paper milk carton. Line the inside of the carton with brown parchment paper. Tie together patterned paper straws with a gift tag and tuck inside the carton with the cookies.

PAPER MILK CARTON

PAPER STRAWS

GIFT TAG

CHOCOLATE PIZZELLE

CHOCOLATE PIZZELLE

PREP 1 hour
BAKE according to manufacturer's directions

1½ cups hazelnuts (filberts), toasted*
2¼ cups all-purpose flour
3 Tbsp. unsweetened cocoa powder
1 Tbsp. baking powder
3 eggs
1 cup sugar
⅓ cup butter, melted and cooled
2 tsp. vanilla
1 recipe Chocolate Glaze

1. Finely chop 1 cup of the hazelnuts; set aside. Place remaining ½ cup hazelnuts in a blender or food processor. Cover and blend until very fine but dry and not oily. In a bowl stir together the ground hazelnuts, flour, cocoa powder, and baking powder.
2. In a large mixing bowl beat eggs with a mixer on high 4 minutes or until thick and lemon color. Gradually add sugar, beating on medium. Beat in butter and vanilla until combined. Add flour mixture, beating on low until combined.
3. Heat an electric pizzelle iron according to manufacturer's directions. (Or heat a nonelectric pizzelle iron on stovetop over medium heat until a drop of water sizzles on the grid. Reduce heat to medium low.)
4. For each pizzella, place a slightly rounded tablespoon of batter on pizzelle grid, slightly off-center toward the back. Close lid. Bake according to manufacturer's directions. (For a nonelectric iron, bake 2 minutes or until golden brown, turning once.) Transfer pizzella to a paper towel to cool.
5. Dip the edges of each pizzella into Chocolate Glaze then into the reserved chopped hazelnuts to coat edges. Place pizzelle on wire racks until set. Makes 64 servings.

Chocolate Glaze In a bowl stir together 3 cups powdered sugar, ⅓ cup unsweetened cocoa powder, and 1 tsp. vanilla. Stir in enough milk (4 to 6 Tbsp.) to make dipping consistency.

*Tip Spread hazelnuts in a single layer in a shallow baking pan. Bake in a 325°F oven 15 to 20 minutes or until light golden brown, stirring once or twice; cool completely. Remove papery skins by rubbing with a clean dish towel.

PER SERVING *120 cal., 5 g fat (1 g sat. fat), 22 mg chol., 54 mg sodium, 17 g carb., 1 g fiber, 2 g pro.*

CARAMEL-CASHEW BARS

PREP 15 minutes
BAKE 23 minutes at 325°F

3 cups finely crushed shortbread cookies (63 cookies)
½ cup butter, melted
¼ cup sugar
36 vanilla caramels, unwrapped
½ cup heavy cream
2 cups coarsely chopped cashews or dry-roasted peanuts
2 cups tiny marshmallows

1. Preheat oven to 325°F. Line a 13×9-inch baking pan with foil, extending foil over edges of pan. Lightly grease foil.
2. In a large bowl stir together crushed shortbread cookies, butter, and sugar. Press cookie mixture firmly and evenly in prepared pan. Bake 15 minutes or until crust is golden and dried around edges. Cool in pan on a wire rack.
3. Meanwhile, in a medium heavy saucepan stir caramels and cream over medium-low heat until melted and smooth. Stir in cashews. Sprinkle marshmallows over baked shortbread crust. Pour caramel mixture over marshmallows; carefully spread evenly.
4. Bake 8 to 10 minutes or until caramel is set and bubbly around edges. Cool in pan on a wire rack. Use foil to lift uncut bars out of pan. Place on cutting board; cut into bars. Makes 24 servings.

PER SERVING *317 cal., 18 g fat (8 g sat. fat), 22 mg chol., 245 mg sodium, 34 g carb., 1 g fiber, 4 g pro.*

As a gift Line a shallow box with parchment paper or waxed paper. From brown kraft paper make a gift tag; punch a hole to loop twine through. Using crafts glue, attach cutouts to tag. Label tag; place bars in box. Cover box. Wrap twine around box.

WINDOW BOX

RIBBON TIED INTO A BOW

FELT LEAVES

As a gift Using rub-on decorations found at crafts store, embellish the top edges of the box. Attach felt leaves and ribbon to the lid with crafts glue.

Bake A
BATCH of
Memories

CARAMEL-CASHEW
BARS

PEPPERMINT
BROWNIE PIE

PEPPERMINT BROWNIE PIE

PREP 30 minutes
BAKE 55 minutes at 350°F
COOL 20 minutes

½	cup butter
3	oz. unsweetened chocolate, chopped
1	recipe Pastry for a Single-Crust Pie
3	eggs, lightly beaten
1½	cups sugar
½	cup all-purpose flour
1	tsp. vanilla
1	cup mint-flavor semisweet chocolate pieces
	Whipped cream
	Miniature candy canes (optional)

1. In a small saucepan combine butter and chocolate. Stir over low heat until melted; cool slightly.

2. Meanwhile, preheat oven to 350°F. Prepare Pastry for a Single-Crust Pie. On a lightly floured surface, slightly flatten dough. Roll dough from center to edge into a 12-inch circle. Wrap pastry circle around rolling pin; unroll into a 9-inch pie plate. Ease pastry into pie plate without stretching. Trim pastry to ½ inch beyond edge of pie plate. Fold under extra pastry even with edge of plate. Crimp edge as desired. Do not prick pastry.

3. For filling, in a large bowl combine eggs, sugar, flour, and vanilla. Stir in melted chocolate and the chocolate pieces. Pour filling into pastry-lined pie plate.

4. Bake 55 minutes or until filling is evenly puffed and edge of filling is slightly cracked. Cool on a wire rack 20 minutes or until slightly warm (center will sink slightly as pie cools). Serve with whipped cream and, if desired, top with candy canes. Makes 8 servings.

Pastry for a Single-Crust Pie In a bowl stir together 1¼ cups flour and ½ tsp. salt. Using a pastry blender, cut in ¼ cup shortening and ¼ cup butter, cut up, until pieces are pea size. Sprinkle 1 Tbsp. ice water over part of the flour mixture; toss gently with a fork. Push moistened dough to side of bowl. Repeat with additional ice water, 1 Tbsp. at a time, until all the flour mixture is moistened (use ¼ to ⅓ cup total ice water). Gather into a ball, kneading gently until dough holds together.
PER SERVING *542 cal., 31 g fat (17 g sat. fat), 150 mg sodium, 64 g carb., 3 g fiber, 6 g pro.*

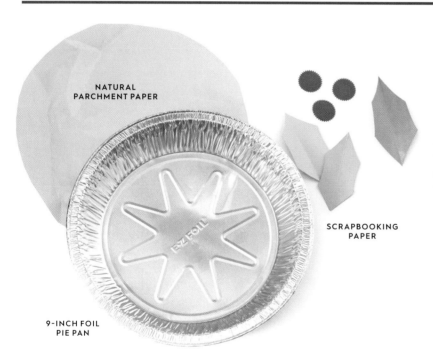

NATURAL
PARCHMENT PAPER

SCRAPBOOKING
PAPER

9-INCH FOIL
PIE PAN

As a gift Trace the top of the pan onto parchment paper; cut out. Cut out about 18 holly leaves from green paper by folding pieces in half to cut symmetrical shapes. Punch out or cut about twenty 1-inch red paper circles for berries. Attach leaves and berries in a 9-inch wreath on parchment circle using crafts glue. To secure wreath to pie pan, attach two to four 1×8-inch strips of paper to opposite sides of the underside of wreath. Place wreath over pie and secure strips to bottom of pie pan with double-stick tape.

SAVORY HERBED BLUE
CHEESE AND WALNUT
SHORTBREADS, 140

BALSAMIC, SHALLOT, AND GOAT CHEESE TART, PAGE 139

New Year's Eve Small Plates

Top off the holiday season with a grown-up gathering featuring elegant appetizers. This collection of small plates—from pâté and savory pastries to black-tie desserts—adds up to big style.

COUNTRY PORK PÂTÉ WITH DRIED APPLES AND PISTACHIOS

PREP 30 minutes
CHILL 5 hours
BAKE 50 minutes at 375°F
COOL 30 minutes

1½   lb. coarsely ground pork*
¼   cup finely snipped dried apple slices
½   cup whole roasted shelled pistachio nuts
¼   cup brandy or Cognac
¼   cup apple juice
1   egg white, lightly beaten
1½   tsp. salt
¼   tsp. black pepper
6   slices bacon
4   bay leaves
    Coarse-ground mustard, cornichons or sour gherkins, and baguette slices

1. In a bowl combine the first eight ingredients (through pepper). Using your hands, mix well. Cover bowl with plastic wrap; chill 1 hour.
2. Preheat oven to 375°F. Using a wooden spoon, firmly press chilled pork mixture against the side of bowl. Discard excess liquid.
3. Line two 5½×3-inch loaf pans crosswise with three slices bacon each (ends of bacon will drape over edges of pans). Divide pork mixture between loaf pans and pat firmly into pans (pans will be full). Place two bay leaves on top of pork mixture in each pan; fold bacon slices over top of bay leaves. Place loaf pans on a foil-lined baking sheet.
4. Bake 50 to 60 minutes or until thermometer inserted in centers registers 170°F. Remove pans from oven; carefully tilt pans over a heatproof bowl to drain excess fat. Place foil over each pan; weight with 1-lb. can to compress pâté. Cool 30 minutes, then refrigerate 4 hours or until fully chilled.
5. Remove cans and foil. Discard bay leaves. Invert loaf pans onto a cutting board. If desired, discard bacon. With a sharp serrated knife, cut each loaf into 12 slices.
6. Serve cold sliced pâté with mustard, cornichons, and baguette slices. Makes 24 servings.
***Tip** Ask your butcher to coarsely grind the pork.
PER SERVING *117 cal., 8 g fat (3 g sat. fat), 22 mg chol., 293 mg sodium, 3 g carb., 0 g fiber, 6 g pro.*

WILD MUSHROOM-STUFFED BEEF TENDERLOIN

PREP 30 minutes
ROAST 40 minutes at 425°F
STAND 10 minutes

1   3½- to 4-lb. center-cut beef tenderloin roast
3   oz. pancetta, chopped
2   Tbsp. olive oil
3   cups chopped assorted fresh wild mushrooms (such as chanterelle, shiitake, and/or oyster mushrooms)
2   shallots, finely chopped
2   cloves garlic, minced
2½   cups soft bread crumbs
3   Tbsp. snipped fresh Italian parsley
¼   cup butter, softened
2   Tbsp. finely shredded Parmesan cheese
2   Tbsp. Dijon mustard
    Sliced assorted fresh wild mushrooms, sautéed (optional)

1. Preheat oven to 425°F. Trim fat from meat. Make a lengthwise cut along center of meat, cutting almost to, but not through, opposite side. Spread open; set aside.
2. For stuffing, in a large skillet cook pancetta in hot oil over medium heat until crisp. Using a slotted spoon, remove and drain pancetta on paper towels, reserving drippings in skillet. Add the 3 cups mushrooms, shallots, and garlic to drippings. Cook until mushrooms and shallots are tender, stirring occasionally. Cool slightly. In a large bowl combine 1½ cups of the bread crumbs and the parsley. Add pancetta and mushroom mixture; toss gently to combine.
3. Spoon stuffing along center of meat. Bring up sides of meat around stuffing, pressing to almost enclose stuffing. Tie at 2-inch intervals with 100%-cotton kitchen string. Place roll, seam side up, on a rack in a shallow roasting pan.
4. In a medium bowl combine butter, cheese, and mustard. Spread over top and sides of meat roll. Press remaining 1 cup bread crumbs onto top and sides of roll.
5. Roast, uncovered, 40 to 45 minutes for medium rare (140°F). Remove from oven. Cover loosely with foil; let stand 10 minutes before slicing (temperature of meat will rise 5°F while it stands).
6. Remove string. Cut roll into ½-inch slices. Serve warm. If desired, serve with sautéed mushrooms. Makes 28 servings.
PER SERVING *136 cal., 8 g fat (3 g sat. fat), 45 mg chol., 153 mg sodium, 3 g carb., 0 g fiber, 14 g pro.*

COUNTRY PORK PÂTÉ WITH DRIED APPLES AND PISTACHIOS

WILD
MUSHROOM-
STUFFED BEEF
TENDERLOIN

HABANERO CHICKEN KABOBS

PREP 35 minutes
COOK 5 minutes
GRILL 6 minutes

35   6- to 8-inch wooden skewers
1   lime
½   cup orange marmalade
⅓   cup water
4   green onions, finely chopped
1   medium carrot, finely shredded
3   Tbsp. canola oil
2   Tbsp. apple cider vinegar
4   cloves garlic, minced
1   fresh habanero pepper, seeded
      and finely chopped (tip, page 29)
1   tsp. ground cumin
⅛   tsp. ground cloves
2   lb. skinless, boneless chicken
      breast halves
¼   cup fresh cilantro leaves

1. Soak wooden skewers in water 20 minutes.
2. Remove 2 tsp. zest and the juice from lime. In a small saucepan combine zest, juice, marmalade, the water, green onions, carrot, oil, vinegar, garlic, habanero pepper, cumin, and cloves. Bring to a boil over medium-high heat. Reduce heat to medium and cook, uncovered, 5 minutes, stirring occasionally. Remove from heat. Place half the sauce into a small bowl.
3. Meanwhile, bias-slice chicken crosswise into ¼-inch thick strips. Thread chicken onto skewers accordion-style. Brush with remaining sauce.
4. Grill kabobs, covered, directly over medium heat 6 minutes (165°F), turning once. Transfer to a platter; top with reserved sauce and cilantro. Makes 35 servings.
PER SERVING *110 cal., 4 g fat (0 g sat. fat), 34 mg chol., 59 mg sodium, 7 g carb., 0 g fiber, 12 g pro.*

BASIL SHRIMP CHOWDER

PREP 20 minutes
COOK 20 minutes

2   Tbsp. butter
1   cup finely chopped celery
1   cup chopped red onion
½   cup finely chopped green sweet
      pepper
2   Tbsp. all-purpose flour
2   cups water
2   8-oz. bottles clam juice
2   tsp. Old Bay seasoning
1   tsp. dried basil, crushed
1½   lb. large shrimp, peeled, tails on
1   12-oz. pkg. frozen whole kernel
      corn
2   Tbsp. capers
1   8-oz. container mascarpone
      cheese
1   recipe Cheesy Polenta (optional)

1. In a large pot melt butter over medium heat. Add celery, onion, and sweet pepper. Cook and stir 5 minutes or until tender. Stir in flour until coated. Add the water, clam juice, Old Bay seasoning, and dried basil. Bring to boiling; reduce heat.
2. Stir in shrimp, corn, and capers. Cook 2 to 5 minutes or until shrimp are bright pink. Remove from heat. Stir in mascarpone cheese until melted. If desired, serve with Cheesy Polenta. Makes 8 servings.
PER SERVING *267 cal., 16 g fat (9 g sat. fat), 167 mg chol., 449 mg sodium, 13 g carb., 2 g fiber, 18 g pro.*

Cheesy Polenta In a large saucepan bring 2½ cups water to boiling. In a medium bowl combine 1 cup white or yellow cornmeal, 1 cup cold water, and ½ tsp. salt. Slowly add cornmeal mixture to boiling water, stirring constantly. Cook and stir until mixture returns to boiling. Reduce heat to low. Cook, uncovered, 10 to 15 minutes or until mixture is very thick, stirring occasionally. Stir in 1 cup shredded sharp cheddar cheese (4 oz.) and ¼ cup milk until cheese is melted. Stir in 1 Tbsp. snipped fresh basil.

CLAMS WITH FRESH HERB BUTTER SAUCE

PREP 40 minutes
COOK 15 minutes

32   to 40 fresh littleneck clams
2   Tbsp. olive oil
¼   tsp. crushed red pepper
1   small leek, cleaned and sliced
¾   cup clam broth or juice
¼   cup dry white wine
1   large tomato, seeded and coarsely
      chopped
¼   cup loosely packed torn or small
      basil leaves
2   Tbsp. snipped fresh Italian parsley
1   Tbsp. snipped fresh oregano
2   cups loosely packed baby arugula
4   Tbsp. butter, at room temperature
      Toasted crusty bread slices

1. Scrub clams well under cold running water; set aside.
2. In a 8-quart heavy-bottom Dutch oven with tight-fitting lid, heat oil over medium-high heat. Add crushed red pepper. Cook and stir 20 seconds. Add sliced leek and cook 3 minutes or just until tender. Add broth and wine; bring to boiling.
3. Add clams to pot. Reduce heat to medium; cover and cook 5 minutes. Use tongs to remove any clams that have opened and transfer them to a serving bowl. Add tomato and cook 5 minutes more or until more clams have opened, removing clams as they open. Discard any clams that do not open.
4. Increase heat to high. Add basil, parsley, and oregano to pot and bring to a boil. Remove from heat; stir in arugula and butter until butter is melted and arugula just begins to wilt. Spoon over clams and serve with bread. Makes 6 servings.
PER SERVING *250 cal., 16 g fat (6 g sat. fat), 43 mg chol., 711 mg sodium, 16 g carb., 1 g fiber, 14 g pro.*

HABANERO
CHICKEN SKEWERS

INDIAN-SPICED
SWEET POTATO
FRITTERS

INDIAN-SPICED SWEET POTATO FRITTERS

PREP 15 minutes
COOK 8 minutes

1   6-oz. container plain whole milk yogurt
2   Tbsp. snipped fresh cilantro
½   tsp. lime zest
⅛   tsp. salt
     Dash cayenne pepper
1   lb. sweet potatoes, peeled and coarsely shredded
¼   cup sliced green onion
½   cup all-purpose flour
1¼   tsp. garam masala
½   tsp. baking powder
½   tsp. salt
¼   tsp. ground cumin
⅛   tsp. black pepper
1   egg, lightly beaten
2   Tbsp. canola oil
     Lime wedges (optional)

1. Preheat oven to 200°F. For yogurt sauce, in a bowl stir together yogurt, cilantro, lime zest, salt, and cayenne pepper.

2. In a bowl combine sweet potatoes and green onion. Add flour, garam masala, baking powder, salt, cumin, and black pepper; toss to coat. Stir in egg until combined.

3. In a large nonstick skillet heat 2 tsp. oil over medium heat. Working in batches, drop batter by slightly rounded tablespoons into the hot skillet. Use a spatula to flatten into patties ½-inch-thick. Cook 4 to 5 minutes per side or until brown. Keep fritters warm in oven while cooking remaining batter, adding more oil as needed.

4. Serve fritters with yogurt sauce and, if desired, lime wedges. Makes 18 servings.

PER SERVING *58 cal., 2 g fat (0 g sat. fat), 12 mg chol., 175 mg sodium, 8 g carb., 1 g fiber, 1 g pro.*

BALSAMIC SHALLOT AND GOAT CHEESE TART

PREP 30 minutes
BAKE 18 minutes at 400°F
STAND 5 minutes

3   Tbsp. butter
8   small shallots, quartered lengthwise
3   Tbsp. honey

BALSAMIC SHALLOT AND GOAT CHEESE TART

3   Tbsp. balsamic vinegar
½   tsp. salt
½   tsp. black pepper
½   17.3-oz. pkg. frozen puff pastry sheets, thawed (1 sheet)
1   egg yolk
2   tsp. water
4   oz. goat cheese (chèvre), broken into small chunks
2   tsp. snipped fresh Italian parsley

1. Preheat oven to 400°F. In a medium ovenproof skillet melt butter over medium heat. Stir in shallots and honey. Cook 10 minutes or until shallots start to brown, stirring occasionally. Stir in balsamic vinegar, salt, and pepper.

2. Transfer skillet to oven. Bake 15 to 20 minutes or until shallots are tender and liquid is syrupy.

3. Meanwhile, on a large baking sheet unfold puff pastry. Trim a ½-inch-wide strip from each side of the pastry. Combine egg yolk and the water. Lightly brush edges of pastry sheet with egg yolk mixture. Place pastry strips on edges of pastry sheet to form a ridge, trimming excess pastry. Lightly brush ridge with egg yolk mixture. Using a fork, generously prick bottom of pastry.

4. Bake 15 to 20 minutes or until pastry is puffed and golden brown. Spread shallot mixture on pastry. (Pastry will sink when topped.) Top with cheese. Bake 3 to 5 minutes more or until cheese is softened. Sprinkle with parsley. Let stand 5 minutes before serving. Makes 9 servings.

PER SERVING *277 cal., 19 g fat (8 g sat. fat), 43 mg chol., 294 mg sodium, 23 g carb., 0 g fiber, 6 g pro.*

**SAVORY HERBED
BLUE CHEESE
AND WALNUT
SHORTBREADS**

SAVORY HERBED BLUE CHEESE AND WALNUT SHORTBREADS

PREP 30 minutes
CHILL 2 hours 35 minutes
BAKE 12 minutes at 325°F
COOL 2 minutes

⅔ cup walnuts
1 cup crumbled blue cheese, at room temperature (4 oz.)
¾ cup butter, softened
1 egg
1½ cups all-purpose flour
2 Tbsp. snipped fresh sage
1¼ to 1½ tsp. cracked black pepper
½ tsp. salt
½ tsp. baking powder
½ cup finely chopped walnuts
1 3-oz. pkg. very thinly sliced prosciutto, cut in thin strips
Small sage leaves and/or thyme sprigs

1. In a food processor pulse walnuts until finely chopped. Add cheese, butter, and egg; cover and process until smooth. Add flour, sage, pepper, salt, and baking powder. Cover and process just until combined. Transfer to a bowl and chill 35 minutes until firm enough to roll into logs.
2. Roll into two 1½-inch diameter logs. On a sheet of waxed paper or parchment paper spread additional ½ cup finely chopped walnuts and roll logs in nuts to coat. Wrap logs with plastic wrap and chill until firm enough to cut (2 to 12 hours).**
3. Preheat oven to 325°F. Cut logs into ¼-inch slices. Place on parchment paper-lined baking sheets. Bake 12 minutes or until lightly browned around edges.

4. Cool on baking sheet 2 minutes. Transfer to cooling racks; cool completely. Top with strips of prosciutto and small sage leaves and/or thyme sprigs. Makes 44 servings.
PER SERVING *81 cal., 6 g fat (3 g sat. fat), 17 mg chol., 149 mg sodium, 4 g carb., 0 g fiber, 2 g pro.*
* For a nice round shape, lay log on parchment or waxed paper. Fold paper over log and use as a guide.
** Logs can be refrigerated 1 to 2 days or frozen up to 3 months. If freezing, wrap tightly and place in freezer bag. Remove from freezer and thaw until soft enough to cut without crumbling (about 10 minutes). Bake as directed, adding 1 to 2 minutes to baking time.

ROASTED RADISHES WITH CHIVE VINAIGRETTE

PREP 15 minutes
ROAST 30 minutes at 425°F

- 1½ lb. radishes, trimmed, scrubbed, and halved
- 3 Tbsp. olive oil
- 2 Tbsp. white wine vinegar
- 1 Tbsp. snipped fresh chives
- ½ tsp. Dijon mustard
- ¼ tsp. black pepper
- ⅛ tsp. salt

1. Preheat oven to 425°F. In a bowl toss radishes with 1 Tbsp. of the olive oil. Place radishes in a 15×10-inch baking pan. Roast, uncovered, 30 to 35 minutes or until tender and lightly browned, stirring once.
2. For vinaigrette, in a screw-top jar combine remaining 2 Tbsp. olive oil and remaining ingredients. Cover and shake well. Drizzle vinaigrette over radishes; toss to coat. Makes 6 servings.
PER SERVING *80 cal., 7 g fat (1 g sat. fat), 0 mg chol., 103 mg sodium, 4 g carb., 2 g fiber, 1 g pro.*

PANKO ROASTED ASPARAGUS

PREP 20 minutes
ROAST 12 minutes at 425°F

- 1 lb. thick asparagus spears
- ½ cup mayonnaise
- ¼ cup Dijon mustard
- 2 tsp. lemon juice
- 1 cup panko bread crumbs
- 2 Tbsp. peanut oil

1. Preheat oven to 425°F. Snap off and discard woody bases from asparagus. In a bowl combine mayonnaise, mustard, and lemon juice. Transfer half the mixture to a serving bowl; cover. Chill until ready to serve.
2. Place bread crumbs in a shallow dish. Spread remaining mayonnaise mixture over asparagus spears; roll in bread crumbs to coat. Place in an ungreased 15×10×1-inch baking pan. Drizzle with oil.
3. Roast 12 minutes or until asparagus is crisp-tender and bread crumbs are golden brown. Serve with reserved mayonnaise mixture. Makes 16 servings.
PER SERVING *88 cal., 7 g fat (1 g sat. fat), 3 mg chol., 139 mg sodium, 4 g carb., 1 g fiber, 1 g pro.*

PANKO ROASTED ASPARAGUS

MACADAMIA
NUT HUMMUS

PEPPERED KALE CHIPS

PREP 10 minutes
BAKE 22 minutes at 300°F

1   bunch fresh kale
1   Tbsp. olive oil
¼   tsp. salt
¼   tsp. coarsely ground black pepper
⅛   tsp. cayenne pepper (optional)

1. Preheat oven to 300°F. Line two large baking sheets with parchment paper.
2. Remove and discard thick stems from kale. Tear leaves into bite-size pieces. Rinse and dry in a salad spinner or pat dry with paper towels.
3. In a large bowl combine kale, oil, salt, black pepper, and, if desired, cayenne pepper. Massage kale with your hands to thoroughly coat. Arrange in a single layer on prepared baking sheets. Bake 20 minutes. Stir gently. Bake 2 to 4 minutes more or until completely dry and crisp. Makes 4 servings.
PER SERVING *73 cal., 4 g fat (1 g sat. fat), 0 mg chol., 182 mg sodium, 9 g carb., 2 g fiber, 3 g pro.*
To Store Store cooled chips in an airtight container. If necessary, recrisp chips in a 325°F oven 3 to 4 minutes.

MACADAMIA NUT HUMMUS

PREP 20 minutes
STAND 7 hours

1½   cups unsalted raw macadamia nuts
1   lemon
½   cup water
¼   cup olive oil
3   Tbsp. tahini (sesame seed paste)
2   cloves garlic, minced
¼   tsp. sea salt
¼   tsp. cayenne pepper (optional)
     Cut-up vegetables (such as carrots, celery, sweet peppers, zucchini, and/or summer squash)
     Paprika (optional)

1. In a medium bowl combine nuts and enough water to cover. Let stand, covered, 7 to 24 hours; drain. (To quick-soak, cover nuts with boiling water and let stand 10 minutes; drain). Rinse and drain again. Meanwhile, remove 1 tsp. zest and squeeze 3 Tbsp. juice from lemon.
2. In a food processor combine nuts, lemon zest and juice, the water, oil,

tahini, garlic, salt, and cayenne pepper. Cover and process 4 to 5 minutes or until smooth. If desired, chill hummus.
3. Drizzle with additional oil and sprinkle with additional cayenne or paprika, if desired. Serve with cut-up vegetables. Store in refrigerator up to 3 days. Makes 20 servings.
PER SERVING *110 cal., 12 g fat (2 g sat. fat), 0 mg chol., 29 mg sodium, 2 g carb., 1 g fiber, 1 g pro.*

SPICY EDAMAME DIP

PREP 15 minutes
COOK 7 minutes
CHILL 1 hour

1   lb. fresh or frozen sweet soybeans (edamame)
¼   cup packed fresh cilantro leaves
2   Tbsp. chopped red onion
2   Tbsp. lime juice
2   tsp. sriracha sauce
1   clove garlic, sliced
¼   tsp. kosher salt
     Assorted cut-up vegetables

1. In a medium saucepan cook edamame in a large amount of boiling water 7 minutes. Drain, reserving 1 cup of the cooking liquid; set aside.
2. In a food processor combine cooked edamame, cilantro leaves, onion, lime juice, sriracha, garlic, and kosher salt. Cover and process, slowly pouring in enough reserved cooking liquid to make a smooth dip and scraping down sides as needed. Cover and chill at least 1 hour before serving.
3. Serve with cut-up vegetables. Cover and chill up to 3 days. Makes 10 servings.
PER SERVING *73 cal., 3 g fat (0 g sat. fat), 0 mg chol., 83 mg sodium, 8 g carb., 4 g fiber, 6 g pro.*

SPICY
EDAMAME DIP

GRAHAM CRACKER S'MORE CAKE

PREP 45 minutes
BAKE 23 minutes at 350°F
COOL 10 minutes

1   recipe Chocolate Filling
1⅔ cups finely crushed graham
    crackers (about 28 squares)
¼   cup all-purpose flour
1½ tsp. baking powder
¼   tsp. salt
½   cup shortening
1   cup sugar
½   tsp. vanilla
3   eggs, separated and at room
    temperature
¾   cup milk
½   cup chopped walnuts (optional)
1   recipe Marshmallow Frosting

1. Prepare Chocolate Filling; cover and
set aside. Preheat oven to 350°F. Grease
two 8-inch round cake pans and line with
waxed paper; grease and flour pans and
waxed paper.
2. In a bowl combine graham crackers,
flour, baking powder, and salt. In a large
bowl beat shortening with a mixer on high
about 30 seconds. Add sugar and vanilla,
beating on medium until well combined.

Add egg yolks; beat until combined.
Alternately add flour mixture and milk
to shortening mixture, beating on low
after each addition just until combined. If
desired, stir in nuts.
3. Thoroughly wash beaters. In a large
clean bowl beat egg whites with mixer
on high until stiff peaks form (tips stand
straight). Gently fold about one-third of
the egg whites into batter to lighten. Fold
in remaining egg whites. Spread batter
into prepared pans.
4. Bake 23 to 25 minutes or until a
toothpick comes out clean. Cool cake
layers in pans 10 minutes. Remove layers
from pans; cool on wire racks.
5. Place a cake layer, bottom side up, on a
serving plate. Spread Chocolate Filling on
top of cake to within ¼ inch of edge. Top
with second cake layer, top side up. Frost
sides and top with Marshmallow Frosting.
Store leftover cake in refrigerator. Icing
will lose some fluffiness. Makes 12 servings.
Chocolate Filling In a small saucepan
bring ½ cup heavy cream just to boiling
over medium-high heat. Remove
from heat. Add 6 oz. semisweet
chocolate pieces (do not stir). Let stand
5 minutes. Stir until smooth. Let stand
at room temperature until ready to
assemble cake.
Marshmallow Frosting In the top of a
2-quart double-boiler combine 1 cup
sugar, ¼ cup cold water, 2 egg whites,
and ¼ tsp. cream of tartar. Beat with a
mixer on low 30 seconds. Place pan over
boiling water (upper pan should not touch
the water). Cook, beating constantly
with mixer on high, for 10 to 13 minutes
or until an instant-read thermometer
registers 160°F, stopping mixer and
quickly scraping pan every 5 minutes to
prevent sticking. Remove from heat; add
1 tsp. vanilla. Beat about 1 minute more or
until frosting is fluffy and soft peaks form
(tips curl).
PER SERVING *417 cal., 20 g fat (8 g sat. fat),
63 mg chol., 223 mg sodium, 59 g carb.,
2 g fiber, 5 g pro.*

UPSIDE-DOWN GRAPEFRUIT CAKES

PREP 30 minutes
BAKE 25 minutes at 400°F
COOL 10 minutes

2   to 3 grapefruits
⅓   cup granulated sugar
¼   cup butter, melted
1¼ cups all-purpose flour
1   cup granulated sugar
1   tsp. baking powder
¼   tsp. salt
¾   cup unrefined coconut oil, melted
2   eggs, lightly beaten
1   tsp. vanilla bean paste or vanilla
    Mint leaves (optional)
    Powdered sugar (optional)

1. Preheat oven to 400°F. Lightly grease
six 8-oz. ramekins or 6-oz. custard cups.
Line a shallow baking pan with foil;
arrange prepared dishes in pan.
2. Peel and remove pith and seeds from
one or two of the grapefruits and cut into
¼-inch slices (you will need 6 slices). Place
one grapefruit slice into the bottom of
each prepared dish. Squeeze ½ cup of
juice from remaining grapefruit; set aside.
In a bowl stir together ⅓ cup sugar and
melted butter until nearly smooth; spoon
over slices in dishes.
3. In a large bowl combine flour, 1 cup
sugar, baking powder, and salt; make a
well in center and set aside. In a medium
bowl combine reserved grapefruit juice,
oil, eggs, and vanilla. Add juice mixture to
flour mixture, stirring to combine. Divide
batter among ramekins. Bake 25 to
30 minutes or until a toothpick inserted in
centers comes out clean. Cool in ramekins
10 minutes. Loosen sides and invert onto
plates. Serve warm, topped with mint
and powdered sugar, if desired. Makes
6 servings.
PER SERVING *631 cal., 37 g fat (29 g
sat. fat), 32 mg chol., 270 mg sodium,
74 g carb., 2 g fiber, 5 g pro.*

GRAHAM CRACKER
S'MORE CAKE

UPSIDE-DOWN
GRAPEFRUIT CAKES

Guest-Worthy Fare

When you think of holiday meals, the big fancy feast may come to mind first, but what about casual fare for feeding out-of-town family and friends who are bunking at your house? These quick-to-fix foods—30-minute dinners, soups, sandwiches, salads, and a slow-cooker risotto—fit into your busy schedule.

ROASTED PEAR HAM MELT,
PAGE 151

147

PORK MEDALLIONS WITH FENNEL AND PANCETTA

START TO FINISH 30 minutes

12   oz. pork tenderloin
¼   cup all-purpose flour
     Dash salt
     Dash black pepper
2   Tbsp. olive oil
2   oz. pancetta or bacon, finely chopped
2   fennel bulbs, trimmed and cut crosswise into ¼-inch slices
1   small onion, thinly sliced
2   cloves garlic, minced
2   Tbsp. lemon juice
½   cup heavy cream
2   Tbsp. snipped fresh Italian parsley

1. Trim fat from tenderloin. Cut crosswise into 1-inch slices. Place each slice between two pieces of plastic wrap. Use the flat side of a meat mallet to lightly pound slices to ¼-inch thickness. Remove plastic wrap.
2. In a shallow dish combine flour, salt, and pepper. Dip slices in flour mixture to coat. In a large heavy skillet heat oil over medium-high heat. Cook pork, half at a time, in hot oil 2 to 3 minutes or until slightly pink in center, turning once. (Add more oil during cooking, if necessary.) Remove medallions from skillet; set aside.
3. In the same skillet cook pancetta over medium-high heat until crisp. Add fennel, onion, and garlic; cook 3 to 5 minutes or until crisp-tender. Add lemon juice; stir in heavy cream. Bring to boiling; return medallions to skillet. Cook until heated through and sauce is slightly thickened.
4. Transfer medallions to a serving platter; top with vegetables and sauce. Sprinkle with parsley. Makes 4 servings.
PER SERVING *382 cal., 24 g fat (10 g sat. fat), 106 mg chol., 416 mg sodium, 18 g carb., 4 g fiber, 23 g pro.*

CHARRED SWEET PEPPERS POTATO CHOWDER

PREP 20 minutes
COOK 35 minutes

3   cups chopped red sweet peppers
     Nonstick cooking spray
2   cups chopped yellow onions
10   oz. russet potato, peeled and chopped
½   cup vegetable broth
2   cups milk
⅛   tsp. cayenne pepper (optional)
1   Tbsp. butter
¼   cup chopped fresh parsley
     Salt
     Black pepper
½   cup shredded white or sharp cheddar cheese (optional)
¼   cup plain Greek yogurt (optional)
     Crumbled bacon (optional)

1. Coat a 4-qt. Dutch oven with nonstick cooking spray and heat over medium-high heat. Add peppers; coat with cooking spray. Cook, uncovered, 15 minutes or until charred, stirring frequently.
2. Add onions and cook 5 to 6 minutes or until soft and golden brown, stirring occasionally. Stir in potatoes and broth. Bring to boiling, reduce heat, and simmer, covered, 12 minutes or until potatoes are very tender.
3. Coarsely mash with a potato masher. Add the milk and cayenne pepper, if using. Heat through.
4. Remove from heat; stir in butter and parsley and season to taste with salt and pepper. If desired, top servings with cheese, yogurt, and/or bacon. Makes 4 servings.
PER SERVING *255 cal., 11 g fat (6 g sat. fat), 32 mg chol., 284 mg sodium, 30 g carb., 5 g fiber, 11 g pro.*

PORK MEDALLIONS WITH FENNEL AND PANCETTA

ROASTED KALE, TOMATO,
AND CHICKPEA SALAD WITH
WHEAT BERRIES

ROASTED KALE, TOMATO, AND CHICKPEA SALAD WITH WHEAT BERRIES

PREP 15 minutes
COOK 45 minutes
ROAST 30 minutes at 350°F

1	**cup water**
¾	**tsp. salt**
⅓	**cup wheat berries**
¼	**cup olive oil**
2	**cloves garlic, minced**
¾	**tsp. dried oregano, crushed**
¼	**tsp. cayenne pepper**
4	**cups stemmed, chopped kale**
4	**roma tomatoes, quartered lengthwise**
1	**medium red onion, halved lengthwise and sliced ¼ inch thick**
1	**15-oz. can chickpeas (garbanzo beans), rinsed and drained**
1	**Tbsp. lemon juice**
¼	**cup shaved Parmesan cheese**

1. Preheat oven to 350°F. In a small saucepan bring the water and ¼ tsp. of the salt to boiling. Add wheat berries. Reduce heat and simmer, covered, 45 to 60 minutes or until tender but still chewy.
2. Meanwhile, in a small bowl combine olive oil, the remaining ½ tsp. salt, garlic, oregano and cayenne. Place kale in a 15×10×1-inch baking pan. Combine tomatoes, onion, and chickpeas in another 15×10×1-inch baking pan. Drizzle both kale and tomato mixture with 1 Tbsp. oil mixture; toss to coat. Roast, uncovered, 8 minutes for kale (or until edges are brown) and 30 minutes for tomato mixture (or until tomatoes begin to shrink and onion and chickpeas begin to brown), stirring once.
3. Drain and discard excess liquid from wheat berries (if needed) and transfer to a shallow salad bowl. Add kale and tomato mixture. Add lemon juice to remaining 2 Tbsp. oil mixture; whisk to combine. Drizzle salad with dressing; toss. Season to taste with salt and pepper; top with Parmesan cheese. Serve warm or at room temperature. Makes 4 servings.
PER SERVING *341 cal., 18 g fat (3 g sat. fat), 4 mg chol., 822 mg sodium, 38 g carb., 5 g fiber, 13 g pro.*

ROASTED PEAR HAM MELT

ROASTED PEAR HAM MELT

PREP 20 minutes
ROAST 20 minutes at 425°F
COOK 2 minutes

4	**pears, cored and cut lengthwise into ½-inch thick slices**
2	**Tbsp. olive oil**
8	**½-inch thick white bread slices**
½	**cup red pepper jelly**
8	**oz. thinly sliced ham**
4	**slices white cheddar cheese**

1. Preheat oven to 425°F. In a large shallow baking pan toss pear slices with oil. Roast 20 to 25 minutes or until very tender. Cool slightly.

2. Spread all bread slices with pepper jelly. Layer four of the bread slices with ham, roasted pear slices, and cheese. Top with remaining bread slices, spread sides down. Brush both sides of each sandwich with additional olive oil.

3. Heat a large skillet or griddle over medium heat. Cook sandwiches 2 to 3 minutes or until bottoms are golden and cheese is melted, turning once. Makes 4 servings.
PER SERVING *709 cal., 22 g fat (7 g sat. fat), 54 mg chol., 1,286 mg sodium, 106 g carb., 9 g fiber, 24 g pro.*

GREEN SALAD WITH GRAPEFRUIT AND AVOCADO

START TO FINISH 30 minutes

1   very large ruby red grapefruit
2   5-oz. pkg. mixed baby greens
2   avocados, halved, seeded, peeled, and sliced
2   green onions, thinly sliced
¼   cup fresh lemon juice
1   Tbsp. Dijon mustard
½   tsp. sea salt
½   tsp. freshly ground black pepper
⅔   cup extra-virgin olive oil
½   cup roasted, salted pistachios, coarsely chopped

1. Segment grapefruit over a small bowl to catch juices. Reserve 2 Tbsp. juice for dressing.
2. In a large salad bowl toss together greens, avocados, grapefruit segments, and green onions.
3. For dressing, in a bowl whisk together lemon juice, mustard, reserved grapefruit juice, salt, and pepper. Drizzle oil in a thin steady stream into dressing, whisking constantly.
4. Lightly dress salad with some of the dressing; pass remaining dressing. Sprinkle salad with pistachios. Makes 10 servings.
PER SERVING *224 cal., 22 g fat (3 g sat. fat), 0 mg chol., 187 mg sodium, 8 g carb., 3 g fiber, 3 g pro.*

SPINACH-BASIL BROWN RICE RISOTTO

PREP 20 minutes
SLOW COOK 4 hours (low) or 2 hours (high)

    Nonstick cooking spray
1½   cups uncooked brown rice
1   cup chopped red or green sweet pepper
¾   tsp. salt
3½   cups water
2   cups packed fresh spinach, coarsely chopped
¼   to ½ cup snipped fresh basil
¼   cup pine nuts or slivered almonds, toasted (tip, page 20)
2   Tbsp. olive oil
1   tsp. lemon zest
1   clove garlic, minced
    Fresh basil (optional)
    Lemon zest (optional)

1. Coat a 4-quart slow cooker with cooking spray. In prepared cooker combine rice, sweet pepper, and salt. Pour the water over mixture in cooker.
2. Cover and cook on low 4 to 5 hours or high 2 to 2½ hours or until rice is tender.
3. Add spinach, snipped basil, pine nuts, oil, 1 tsp. lemon zest, and garlic to risotto in cooker, stirring until spinach is wilted. If desired, top with additional basil and lemon zest. Makes 10 servings.
PER SERVING *158 cal., 6 g fat (1 g sat. fat), 0 mg chol., 188 mg sodium, 23 g carb., 2 g fiber, 3 g pro.*

GREEN SALAD WITH GRAPEFRUIT AND AVOCADO

SPINACH-BASIL
BROWN RICE
RISOTTO

SWEET AND SALTY
BACON BARS

SWEET AND SALTY BACON BARS

PREP 15 minutes
BAKE 25 minutes at 350°F
COOL 1 hour

½ cup butter
1½ cups finely crushed plain kettle-cooked potato chips (6 oz.)
2 cups semisweet chocolate pieces
12 slices bacon, crisp-cooked and crumbled
1 cup butterscotch-flavor pieces
1 cup shredded coconut
1 cup chopped almonds
1 14-oz. can sweetened condensed milk

1. Preheat oven to 350°F. Line a 13x9-inch baking pan with foil, extending foil beyond edges of pan. Place the butter in the pan and place pan in oven. Bake 5 minutes or until butter is melted.
2. Sprinkle potato chips over butter. Sprinkle with chocolate pieces, bacon, butterscotch pieces, coconut, and almonds. Drizzle condensed milk over layers.
3. Bake 25 to 30 minutes or until edges are light brown. Cool in pan on a wire rack. Use foil to lift uncut bars out of pan. Cut into bars. Makes 32 servings.
PER SERVING *229 cal., 14 g fat (8 g sat. fat), 15 mg chol., 122 mg sodium, 24 g carb., 1 g fiber, 4 g pro.*
To Store Layer bars between sheets of waxed paper in an airtight container; cover. Store in refrigerator up to 3 days. Or wrap individual bars in plastic wrap. Place in an airtight container or resealable plastic freezer bag. Freeze up to 3 months.

PEAR-PECAN CRISP

PREP 20 minutes
BAKE 35 minutes at 375°F
COOL 20 minutes

6 medium pears, just ripe
¼ cup pure maple syrup
2 Tbsp. white whole wheat flour
¼ tsp. ground nutmeg
¼ tsp. ground cardamom
⅛ tsp. salt
½ cup chopped pecans
⅓ cup rolled oats
2 Tbsp. butter, melted

PEAR-PECAN CRISP

2 Tbsp. pure maple syrup
¼ tsp. ground cinnamon
2 cups low-fat vanilla ice cream (optional)

1. Preheat oven to 375°F. Quarter, core, and thinly slice pears. In a large bowl toss together pear slices and the ¼ cup maple syrup. Sprinkle with flour, nutmeg, cardamom, and salt. Toss to combine. Transfer to a 2-qt. rectangular baking dish. Cover with foil; bake 10 minutes.
2. Meanwhile, in a bowl stir together pecans, oats, butter, the 2 Tbsp. syrup, and cinnamon. Uncover pear mixture; spoon pecan mixture over pears.
3. Bake, uncovered, 25 to 30 minutes or until filling is bubbly and topping is lightly browned. Cool in dish on a wire rack 20 minutes. Serve warm. If desired, serve with ice cream. Makes 8 servings.
Tip If desired, substitute 6 large baking apples for pears. In Step 1, increase initial bake time to 20 minutes.
PER SERVING *201 cal., 8 g fat (2 g sat. fat), 8 mg chol., 65 mg sodium, 34 g carb., 5 g fiber, 2 g pro.*

Index